The British Armed Forces

Editor: Tracy Biram

Volume 356

Independence Educational Publishers

First published by Independence Educational Publishers

The Studio, High Green

Great Shelford

Cambridge CB22 5EG

England

ISBN-13: 978 1 86168 812 5

Printed in Great Britain

Zenith Print Group

Contents

Introduction

The British Armed Forces is Volume 356 in the *ISSUES* series. The aim of the series is to offer current, diverse information about important issues in our world, from a UK perspective.

ABOUT THE BRITISH ARMED FORCES

With more people leaving the Armed Forces than are joining, the forces are facing a recruitment crisis. In this book we look at the issues faced by military personnel in their service, and those that can affect veterans when they return to 'civvy street'. We also look at public opinion of the forces and what is being done to improve the lives of the forces.

OUR SOURCES

Titles in the *ISSUES* series are designed to function as educational resource books, providing a balanced overview of a specific subject.

The information in our books is comprised of facts, articles and opinions from many different sources, including:

◆ Newspaper reports and opinion pieces

◆ Website factsheets

◆ Magazine and journal articles

◆ Statistics and surveys

◆ Government reports

◆ Literature from special interest groups.

A NOTE ON CRITICAL EVALUATION

Because the information reprinted here is from a number of different sources, readers should bear in mind the origin of the text and whether the source is likely to have a particular bias when presenting information (or when conducting their research). It is hoped that, as you read about the many aspects of the issues explored in this book, you will critically evaluate the information presented.

It is important that you decide whether you are being presented with facts or opinions. Does the writer give a biased or unbiased report? If an opinion is being expressed, do you agree with the writer? Is there potential bias to the 'facts' or statistics behind an article?

ASSIGNMENTS

In the back of this book, you will find a selection of assignments designed to help you engage with the articles you have been reading and to explore your own opinions. Some tasks will take longer than others and there is a mixture of design, writing and research-based activities that you can complete alone or in a group.

FURTHER RESEARCH

At the end of each article we have listed its source and a website that you can visit if you would like to conduct your own research. Please remember to critically evaluate any sources that you consult and consider whether the information you are viewing is accurate and unbiased.

Useful Websites

www.child-soldiers.org

www.elitebusinessmagazine.co.uk

www.fullfact.org

www.gov.uk

www.hrmagazine.co.uk

www.independent.co.uk

www.inews.co.uk

www.nhs.uk

www.parliament.uk

www.pathfinderinternational.co.uk

www.politicshome.com

www.ssafa.org.uk

www.telegraph.co.uk

www.theconversation.com

www.theguardian.com

www.themilitarytimes.co.uk

www.ukdefencejournal.org.uk

www.yougov.co.uk

Chapter 1

UK Defence Personnel Statistics

An extract from UK Defence Personnel Statistics Briefing paper.

By Noel Dempsey

Understanding military personnel statistics

There are three main ways to measure the number of military personnel (also known as strength): the total full-time UK Armed Forces, total full-time trained UK Armed Forces, or the total full-time UK Regular Forces.

The total full-time UK Armed Forces is the most comprehensive of the three measures. It comprises trained and untrained members of the UK Regular Forces, Gurkhas, and full-time reserve service personnel (FTRS).

The total full-time trained UK Armed Forces is perhaps the most important measure as this is what the 2015 Strategic Defence and Security Review (2015 SDSR) personnel targets are based on.

The 2015 SDSR targets

The 2015 SDSR indicated that the required number of full-time trained UK Armed Forces personnel by 2020 would be 144,200.

The 2015 SDSR also re-affirmed the Government's commitment to increase the size of the trained strength of the reserve forces (known as Future Reserves 2020) to 35,060 personnel.

Trained strength (or trade-trained strength in the Army) comprises military personnel who have completed Phase 1 and Phase 2 training:

Phase 1 includes all new entry training to provide basic military skills.

2015 SDSR strength targets

Trained strength targets of the full-time UK Armed Forces and Future Reserves 2020 by 2020

	Full-time	Reserve
Royal Navy/Royal Marines	30,450	3,100
Army	82,000	30,100
Royal Air Force	31,175	1,860
Total	**144,200**	**35,060**

Source: MOD, SDSR 2015 Defence Key Facts

Phase 2 includes initial individual specialisation, sub-specialisation and technical training following Phase 1 prior to joining the (trade) trained strength.

UK Armed Forces

The total strength of the full-time UK Armed Forces (trained and untrained) at 1 April 2019 was just under 153,000. Most personnel were within the Army (56%) with the remainder being equally split between the Royal Navy/Royal Marines and the RAF.

Across all services there were 29,530 Officers (19%) and 123,426 personnel with other ranks (81%). The distribution of Officers to other ranks varied across each service: around a quarter of all RAF personnel were an officer (24%) compared to less than a fifth (17%) in the Army.

Trained strength

As at 1 April 2019 all branches of the UK Armed Forces were below the 2015 SDSR target for 2020. The full-time trained strength of the UK Armed Forces was 134,304 which is a shortfall of 9,896 (7%). The Army had the largest proportional shortfall (8%) and the Royal Navy/Royal Marines the smallest (4%).

UK Regular Forces diversity

Data on the diversity is published twice a year and focuses on the diversity of the UK Regular Forces rather than the wider UK Armed Forces.

Gender

At 1 October 2018 there were 15,260 women in the UK Regular Forces and accounted for 11% of the total trained and untrained strength.

The proportion of women in the UK Regular Forces has increased over the past few years. At 1 April 1990 women accounted for around 6% of the total UK Regular Forces; by 1 April 2000 this proportion was around 8%. Since 2000 the share of women in the Regular Forces has increased almost every year.

The 2015 SDSR stated that by 2020 at least 15% of the intake to the UK Regular Forces should be female. In the 12 months to 30 September 2018, 11% of the total intake was female.

On 8 July 2016 David Cameron (the then Prime Minister) announced that women would be allowed to serve in close combat roles by 2018. This was achieved on the 25 October 2018 arhen Defence Secretary Gavin Williamson announced that all roles in the military are open to women.

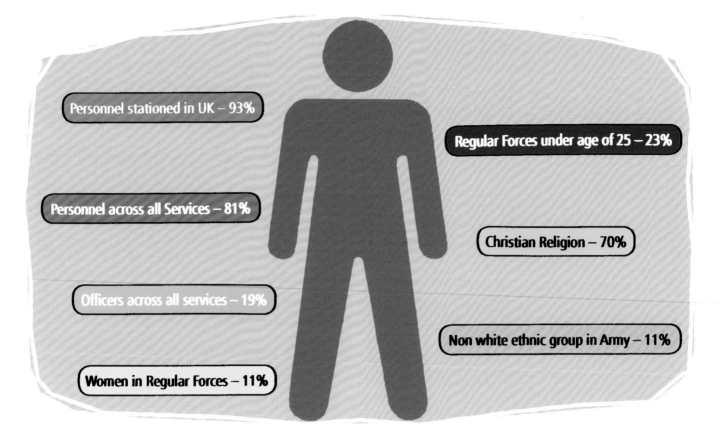

Personnel stationed in UK – 93%

Regular Forces under age of 25 – 23%

Personnel across all Services – 81%

Christian Religion – 70%

Officers across all services – 19%

Non white ethnic group in Army – 11%

Women in Regular Forces – 11%

Ethnicity

As of 1 October 2018 around 8% of personnel (10,950) identified as belonging to a non-white ethnic group. The Army had the highest proportion (11%), followed by the Royal Navy/Marines (4%) and RAF (2%). As with women, the total proportion of non-white ethnic groups personnel across the UK Regular Forces has increased over recent years: on 1 April 2000 around 1% of personnel identified as belonging to a non-white ethnic group.

The 2015 SDSR stated that by 2020 at least 10% of the intake to the UK Regular Forces should be personnel belonging to a non-white ethnic group. In the 12 months to 20 September 2018, 6% of total intake were personnel from a non-white ethnic group.

Age

At 1 October 2018 23% of UK Regular Forces personnel were under the age of 25. The average age of all officers was 37, while the average age of all other ranks was 30. The overall average age was 31.

Religion

At 1 October 2018 70% of UK Regular Forces personnel declared a Christian religion. Around 28% of personnel declared no religion. The next largest religion declared was Hindu (1%) followed by Islam (0.4%). Other faiths (Druid, Pagan, Rastafarian, Spiritualist, Zoroastrian, Wicca, Baha'i and others) accounted for 0.7%.

Location of personnel

The Ministry of Defence publish annual data on the stationed location of trained and untrained UK Regular Forces personnel.

As at 1 April 2018 most personnel were stationed in the United Kingdom (around 93%). Of those stationed overseas the majority were in Europe (5%), followed by North America (0.8%) and North Africa and the Middle East (0.6%). A small proportion of personnel (0.6%) were stationed elsewhere in the world.

Within Europe (excluding the United Kingdom) most personnel were in Germany (3,350) and Cyprus (2,300). Around 900 personnel were stationed in Belgium, Gibraltar, Italy, the Netherlands, Portugal, Norway, France and the Czech Republic.

Following the 2010 Strategic Defence and Security Review there has been a withdrawal of the UK's personnel presence from Germany (a reduction of 15,500) with the aim to completely remove personnel by 2020.

As at 1 April 2018, of those personnel stationed in the United Kingdom the large majority were in England (90%), 7% were stationed in Scotland, 2% were in Wales and 1% were in Northern Ireland. The most notable variations from these proportions among individual branches were that 13% of Royal Navy/Royal Marine personnel were in Scotland, and 3% of the Army were in Northern Ireland (with the Army accounting for 96% of all personnel present in Northern Ireland).

16 May 2019

Are the troops heroes? Americans, Britons and Germans feel very differently

Brits are split between those who think all in the armed are heroes and those who think only those who perform particularly brave acts are.

By Matthew Smith

Ever since 2009, the UK has celebrated Armed Forces Day on the last Saturday in June. The event, itself an extension of the three year old Veterans Day celebration, was implemented to raise awareness and appreciation for those who serve in Britain's armed forces.

Members of the armed forces – especially in the United States, but also in Britain – are often referred to as heroes. But a BBC documentary in 2015 uncovered that many veterans feel uncomfortable with being described as heroes.

Now a new YouGov study conducted in the United States, Great Britain and Germany uncovers drastically different attitudes in each country towards which troops, if any, people consider to be heroes.

The survey asked which members of the armed forces, if any, should be considered heroes. The response is most unified in the US: 50% of Americas say that everyone serving in the armed forces is a hero, regardless of their role or experience.

Britons are split. One-third (32%) also consider all armed forces personnel to be heroes, while an opposing third (31%) believe that only those armed forces personnel who have performed particularly brave acts should be described as heroes.

In Germany, the most common response was that no members of the armed forces should be described as heroes. Three out of every ten Germans (30%) gave this answer. By contrast, only 5% of Americans and 6% of Britons said the same.

In Britain and Germany younger people are the most likely to consider all troops heroes; in the US it is the over-40s

In the US older Americans are most likely to describe all troops as heroes, while younger Americans are less sure. Among Americans aged 40 and over, 55-57% say that all armed forces personnel should be described as heroes, compared to 44% of 30-39 year olds and 37% of 18-29 year olds.

For their part, younger Americans were more likely to answer either that only those serving in combat roles should be described as heroes (12–16% of the under-40s compared to 6–7% of the over-50s), or simply answered 'don't know' (16–21% of the under-40s compared to 5–8% of those aged 50+).

By contrast, in the UK and Germany it is the younger generations who are most likely to believe that all who serve in the armed forces are heroes. In the UK 39% of 18-29 year olds gave this answer – a figure which fell with every age group down to 27% of 60+ year olds. In Germany the figures are 25% of 18–29 year olds falling to 7% of 60+ year olds.

The motivations of older generations in the two countries are different, however. In Britain, older people are more likely to answer that only those troops who had performed brave acts should be described as heroes (37%). In Germany, by contrast, 60+ year olds are most likely to say that no members of the armed forces should be described as heroes

Are the troops heroes? Britons, Germans and Americans answer very differently

Armed forces personnel are often described as heroes. Which ONE of the following comes closest to your view on which armed forces, if any, should be described as heroes?

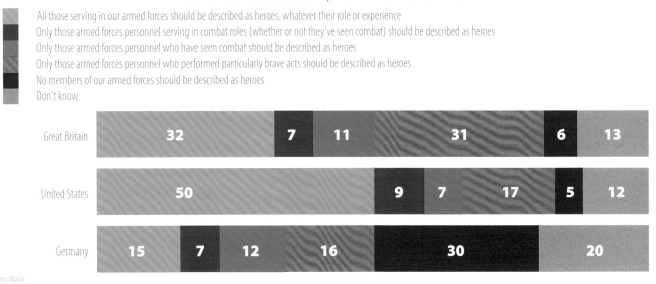

All those serving in our armed forces should be described as heroes, whatever their role or experience
Only those armed forces personnel serving in combat roles (whether or not they've seen combat) should be described as heroes
Only those armed forces personnel who have seen combat should be described as heroes
Only those armed forces personnel who performed particularly brave acts should be described as heroes
No members of our armed forces should be described as heroes
Don't know

	All serving	Combat roles	Seen combat	Brave acts	No members	Don't know
Great Britain	32	7	11	31	6	13
United States	50	9	7	17	5	12
Germany	15	7	12	16	30	20

Source: YouGov

In Britain and Germany younger people are the most likely to say all in the armed forces are heroes – but in the US it is the over-40s

% of those who said 'All those serving in our armed forces should be described as heroes, whatever their role or experience.'

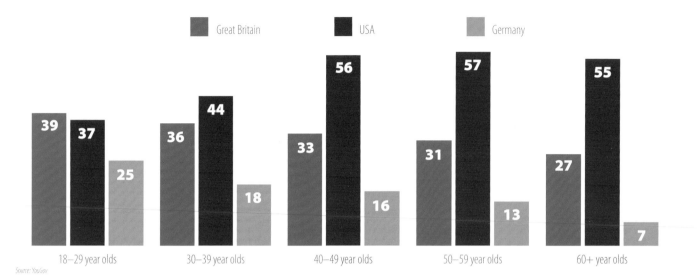

■ Great Britain   ■ USA   ■ Germany

	18–29 year olds	30–39 year olds	40–49 year olds	50–59 year olds	60+ year olds
Great Britain	39	36	33	31	27
USA	37	44	56	57	55
Germany	25	18	16	13	7

Source: YouGov

(44%) – no doubt a result of war guilt being more present among older Germans.

In the UK the divide seems to be more between Remainers and Leavers than along traditional party lines, with little difference between the views of Labour and Conservative voters (although Liberal Democrats are markedly different). Leave voters are more likely to describe all troops as heroes (36% vs 25% of Remain voters), while Remain voters were more likely to say that only those in the armed forces who have performed particularly brave acts are heroes (37% vs 28% of Leavers).

In Germany, AfD voters are the least likely to say that none of the troops are heroes, at 22%, and are the only group for whom this answer is not the most commonly given. By contrast, 26% of CDU/CSU say that no troops are heroes, 35% of SPD and 50% of Green.

In the US, Republicans in particular are likely to say that all the troops are heroes, at 59%. Democrats are closer to the national average at 49%, with Independents being less likely at 42%.

American women are much more likely to say all troops are heroes than men

Women in the US are substantially more likely than men to consider all the troops heroes, with a fifteen percentage point gap between the genders (57% of women vs 42% of men).

In the UK, the most notable gender differences are that women are more likely to consider all armed forces personnel as heroes (36% to 28% of men) while men are more likely to say that only those who have performed particularly brave acts are (34% to 28%).

Differences between men and women in Germany are less pronounced, with the largest being that 24% of German women answered 'don't know' compared to 16% of German men.

28 September 2018

Attitudes to heroism and the armed forces, by party

Armed forces personnel are often described as heroes. Which ONE of the following comes closest to your view on which armed forces personnel, if any, should be described as heroes? %

■ All those serving in our armed forces should be described as heroes, whatever their role or experience

■ Only those armed forces personnel serving in combat roles (whether or not they've seen combat) should be described as heroes

■ Only those armed forces personnel who have seen combat should be described as heroes

■ Only those armed forces personnel who performed particularly brave acts should be described as heroes

■ No members of our armed forces should be described as heroes

■ Don't know

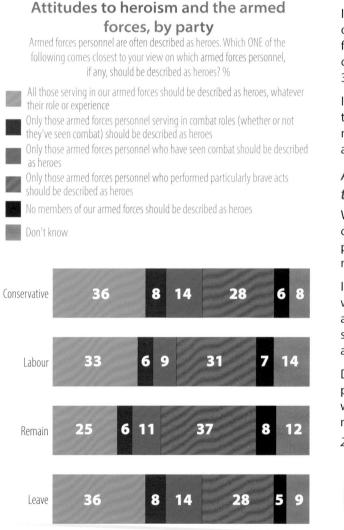

Conservative	36	8	14	28	6	8
Labour	33	6	9	31	7	14
Remain	25	6	11	37	8	12
Leave	36	8	14	28	5	9

Source: YouGov

Armed forces facing biggest shortfall in staff for a decade – report

National Audit Office says five years needed to close gap, with shortage of intelligence analysts.

By Rajeev Syal

The armed forces are experiencing their biggest staffing shortfall for a decade, including a recruitment crisis among intelligence analysts, Whitehall's spending watchdog has said.

A National Audit Office report found the number of full-time military personnel, known as regulars, was 5.7%, or 8,200 people, short of the required level, and that it would take at least five years to close even part of the gap.

The report also highlighted a 26% shortfall in the number of intelligence analysts in the face of the increasing risk of cyber-attacks.

It comes the day after senior security officials in the US and UK held a rare joint conference call to directly blame the Kremlin for targeting government institutions, private sector organisations, infrastructure and internet providers.

Meg Hillier, the chair of the public accounts committee, said the report showed it was critical that Britain had well-staffed armed forces with the technical know-how to handle threats to national security.

'The report shows that the armed forces are woefully below complement, especially in crucial areas like intelligence and engineering. The Ministry of Defence needs to take a long hard look at its current approach,' she said.

Auditors identified 102 trades in the armed services that do not have enough trained regulars to carry out operational tasks. Most of these 'pinch-points' were in six areas – engineering, intelligence, logistics, pilots, communications and medical.

The NAO found a shortfall of 2,400 engineers – with the largest among Royal Navy weapons technicians – 700 intelligence analysts and 800 pilots.

With the impact of the shortfalls becoming more severe over the past year, only six were expected to be resolved in the next five years while 23 would get worse, the report said.

The MoD's plans were 'not a sustainable long-term solution,' it said.

'The department's reliance on a "base-fed" model – where it recruits regulars into the lowest ranks and develops their skills and experience over time – has not enabled it to close capability gaps quickly enough,' the report said.

Each of the three armed services have their own intelligence-gathering teams and recruit their own staff to fill their roles.

The 2015 strategic defence and security review increased the requirement for many intelligence analyst trades. Some within the RAF were required to double or treble recruitment targets in order to meet the new demand.

Demand for intelligence analyst skills, particularly linguists, often changes rapidly depending on emerging threats, but it can take years to train regulars with the skills that are needed.

According to the report, industry and other government intelligence-gathering agencies have targeted and recruited many of these staff.

In response, the MoD has set up specialist recruitment teams and introduced 'retention payments' for those in intelligence roles, the report said.

An MoD spokesman said recruiting and retaining talent was a top priority and that there was a range of schemes used to attract and keep skilled personnel.

'The military has enough personnel to meet all its operational requirements, including being active on 25 operations in 30 countries throughout the world,' he said.

18 April 2018

British Army launches this year's recruitment campaign

The British Army has launched the third and final instalment of its three year 'Belonging' campaign, designed to raise awareness and get young people to consider joining the army for the first time.

By Gerald Wright

Research undertaken by Capita, whom partner with the army in their recruitment endeavours, has shown that only 7% of people know someone who is currently serving whilst a staggering 81% of people have little knowledge of the British Army and its role in society. The campaign for this year consists mainly of three different television adverts; one of a minute in length, and two more each of 30 second duration, and a series of several radio advertisements.

The theme of these are each based around what you would expect of a typical army recruitment advert: transgression and transition of recruits from their role in society based upon the army's ability to see the best in people – typical of the advertisements seen in the last few years. The best example is that of a young lady pushing shopping trolleys for a living where the advert contrasts her current role into one in the army where her characteristics transpose into skills needed of a modern soldier.

Col. Ben Wilde, Asst. Dir of Recruitment said:

'The biggest benefit of joining the army is the sense of belonging experienced amongst soldiers, giving those who serve: common purpose, strong bonds and a sense of working together.'

The campaign takes a gamble with its series of posters on display across the UK consisting of six images based upon a modernisation of the infamous Lord Kitchener 'Your Country Needs You' posters.

The twist being each of the new advertisement posters contains an image of a modern soldier with different phrases including: 'Binge Gamers', 'Class Clowns', 'Snow Flakes', and 'Selfie Addicts' (plus more).

The gamble here is the army are effectively labelling the next generation of soldiers into any one of these categories which could potentially offend new recruits or perhaps miss their target audience where those wishing to join the army do not recognise themselves as fitting into any of the labels identified in the posters.

However, the British Army insists the entire advertisement campaign is focused around 'unlocking potential' and is

designed to illustrate a sense of 'belonging in a team where anyone can do something that matters'.

Notwithstanding this, nobody can fault the British Army for its commitment and resilience in recruitment, especially given the highly competitive marketplace in which it is competing. With unemployment in 16 to 20 year olds being at its lowest for several years, and more younger people travelling as opposed to staying the UK (largely as an effect of globalisation): the British Army ploughs on, and tries to differentiate itself to appear as an appealing option to the next generation of soldiers.

4 January 2019

www.ukdefencejournal.org.uk

Are the UK's armed forces recruiting enough people?

By Claire Milne

The government recently announced that it would be relaxing the rules for Commonwealth citizens wishing to join the UK's armed forces with the aim of increasing the number of Commonwealth recruits to around 1,350 a year.

With that in mind we took a look at what's been happening to armed forces recruitment.

The size of the armed forces is about 9,000 below target

There were just over 192,000 military personnel employed by the UK armed forces as of the start of July 2018. That figure includes the Army, Royal Navy, Marines and Royal Air Force (RAF) as well as the Gurkhas, a division of the Army with Nepalese recruits, and a number of reserve and guard services.

Of these the full-time trained size of the armed forces was around 136,000. That's around 9,000 below the government's target.

The Army has the widest gap between its actual numbers and its target size (around 7%), the RAF is about 6% away from its target, while the Navy and Marines are around 4% away. The combined gap across all forces is about 6%.

Earlier this year the National Audit Office, the public spending watchdog, said that: 'the aggregate figures mask much larger shortfalls in the number of regulars with critical skills, such as engineers, pilots and intelligence analysts.'

More people are leaving the armed forces than joining

We have figures on the numbers joining and leaving the UK Regular Forces each year – that's full-time personnel including nursing services but excluding the Gurkahs, reservists, and some other groups.

In the year to June 2018 around 12,000 personnel joined the UK Regular Forces, and around 15,000 left – altogether a loss of around 3,000 people. In the previous year, almost 13,000 joined and around 15,000 left – a loss of around 2,000 people.

Recent changes to recruitment

The Ministry of Defence has recently made announcements about how recruitment to the armed forces will change.

At the start of November it was announced that the five-year residency requirement for citizens of Commonwealth countries to join the UK's armed forces was being removed– under the new scheme being phased in (over several years) all Commonwealth citizens over the age of 18 can apply. The changes don't apply to people wanting to join the reserves (they will still need to fulfil the residency requirement) and the government said the new rules also won't affect personnel from Ireland or those joining the Gurkhas who have different rules already.

The government hopes that this will increase the number of people from the Commonwealth recruited into the armed forces to 1,350 each year.

The rule about five years of residency was re-introduced in 2013, although from 2016 up to 200 Commonwealth applicants per year who didn't meet the residency requirements could apply to certain posts where there were skills shortages.

In October it was announced that infantry roles in the Army and roles in the Royal Marines were to be opened to women for the first time.

Unlike the new announcement regarding Commonwealth applicants, the government suggests that this isn't really aimed at increasing recruitment, saying that 'the military does not necessarily expect large numbers of women to apply for ground close combat roles'. Instead the changes are aimed at providing equal opportunities for military personnel.

13 November 2018

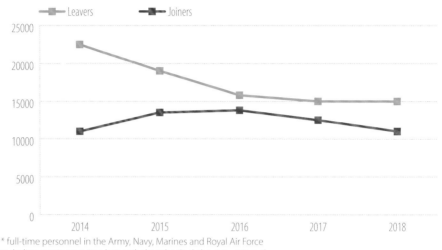

Armed forces leavers and joiners
Intake and outflow from the UK Regular Forces*, as of June each year

— Leavers — Joiners

* full-time personnel in the Army, Navy, Marines and Royal Air Force including nursing services but excluding the Gurkahs, reservists and some other groups.

Source: Ministry of Defence, Quarterly service personnel statistics 2018, Table 4

What would D-Day heroes make of today's snowflake generation?

By Judith Woods

When my children were little and attempted to run through traffic or step heedlessly between parked cars into the road, I would invariably grab them and scold: 'Girls, some things are worth dying for. Freedom, democracy, human rights, that sort of thing; catching a bus is definitely not one of them.'

This week's D-Day commemorations have thrown into sharp relief the servicemen slain in battle 75 years ago in the cause of freedom. Selflessness, courage, a belief that justice must prevail were the forces that drove a generation of young men to lay down their lives so we might live ours in freedom.

Our gaze has necessarily been focused on the past, the pomp, circumstance and pride of victory shot through with grief over fallen comrades and the senseless slaughter that continued even as the Second World War drew to its only possible conclusion.

But as the strains of 'The Last Post' echoed away. I found myself wondering what those brave airmen, sailors and soldiers would think of us, and the 21st-century freedoms we hold so dear.

Would those who landed on Omaha Beach in a hail of German gunfire, death raining down on them salute us for being worthy of their sacrifice?

I'd rather not know the answer, to be quite honest. I'd like to think they would recognise Britain as a tolerant, democratic society, upholding the values they fought for in which equality is the golden standard.

But what would they make of enraged snowflake students calling for 'trigger warnings' over a passage set in the GCSE English exam?

This week, an unseen excerpt from H.E. Bates's classic novel *The Mill* was included in the AQA English Literature test. Later in the book, a character is raped by her employer, so even though the passage made no reference to abuse, its inclusion was enough to spark a hissy fit.

That the 'offending' exam board responded not with the curricular equivalent of a clip round the ear but an apology, would no doubt leave Generation Dunkirk slack-jawed in disbelief.

It is no bad thing that we are less deferential to authority than we were in 1944. Calling power to account is now woven into the fabric of our nation and quite rightly so; what I think those brave, steadfast servicemen would find most shocking is the lack of emotional resilience, moral fibre and sense of duty among their counterparts today.

There has been a profound shift away from shouldering responsibility in favour of demanding rights; every last millennial in the land sees themself as worthy of special treatment, special pleading.

It's all about the individual, never about the group. And if you haven't got any perceptible contribution to make to the world, you can always be offended. Not at man's inhumanity to man – that's a bit heavy for modern sensibilities. Gelatine in bank notes is a good one, or the discriminatory signs on the doors of the Ladies.

Being upset – by a GCSE passage, by other people's opinions, by the need to knuckle down and get on with life – has been elevated to a quasi-religious belief system. Try explaining that to the 6th Airborne Division securing the left flank of Operation Overlord.

The Army is currently around 5,000 short of its 82,500 target of trained soldiers. God knows what Generation Dunkirk would have made of the recent recruitment campaign that targeted 'snowflakes, phone zombies, binge gamers, selfie addicts and me, me, millennials' trapped in 'boring jobs'.

A controversial approach – but it worked. In the first three weeks of January this year, applications to join the army rose to 9,700 – a five-year high.

Which is all well and good, but I'm not sure how I feel about entrusting national security to social media influencers, much less expecting the lactose-intolerant, no-platforming brigade to rise to the challenges of a D-Day scenario.

6 June 2019

1 in 4 Army recruits are teenagers, but experts say new recruits must be over 18 in future

Teenage recruits are vulnerable to self-harm and alcohol misuse.

By Jane Clinton

Experts have warned of the damaging effects on teens serving in the UK army and have called for recruiting children to stop, according to a medical journal editorial.

One in four soldiers in the UK army is under 18. The UK is the only country in Europe and the only permanent member of the UN Security Council to recruit children.

Self-harm

In the editorial in the online journal *BMJ Paediatrics Open*, it says military service for teenagers makes them more vulnerable to self-harm, suicide and alcohol misuse.

These young recruits, often from disadvantaged backgrounds, are more likely to see frontline combat and that, as well as the isolation and culture of military life, can cause harm, they add.

In the UK, 15 year-olds are allowed to begin the enlistment process, with two years of training, starting at the age of 16.

The authors said teen recruitment should stop and welcomed clinicians to support the scrapping of the policy.

Dispute

An Army spokesperson said: 'We strongly dispute many of the assertions in this article, which are based on the assumption that under-18s are deployed on front line combat roles.

'This is not the case as 16 – 18 year old trainee soldiers are not deployed on combat operations and are able to leave employment at any point before their 18th birthday. It is also untrue to suggest we predominantly recruit from disadvantaged backgrounds.

'The Army Foundation College Harrogate has a strong emphasis on training and personnel development, delivering not only formal qualifications but also teaching life-skills such as increased self-esteem and communication skills.'

25 February 2019

The British armed forces: why raising the recruitment age would benefit everyone

Introduction

The British armed forces recruit around 2,300 16- and 17-year-olds each year, of whom four-fifths join the army. This briefing sets out the case for a minimum enlistment age of 18 on grounds of the health, welfare, and rights of minors, and outlines the economic and military benefits of transition to all-adult armed forces.

The UK: an international outlier

Three-quarters of armed forces worldwide now only recruit adults from age 18. Only sixteen states, the UK among them, still formally allow enlistment of 16-year-olds. The UK is the only major military power, the only country in Europe, the only NATO member, and the only Permanent Member of the UN Security Council to do this, recruiting more soldiers at 16 than at any other age.

Widespread criticism

The UK's policy has been challenged by the UN Committee on the Rights of the Child, Parliament's Defence and Human Rights committees, the Children's Commissioners for all four jurisdictions of the UK, the Equality and Human Rights Commission, the major British children's organisations and human rights groups, parliamentarians across the spectrum, faith groups, health professionals, and veterans. A 2018 ICM poll found that 72 percent of respondents who expressed a view said the enlistment age should be 18 or above; only 19 percent thought it should be 16.

Adolescent susceptibilies, weak safeguards

The capacity to make consequential decisions responsibly is reduced in mid-adolescence, particularly among young people from adverse backgrounds. Despite the army's legal duty to ensure that a minor's decision to enlist is fully informed, recruitment materials glamorise military life while omitting its risks and complex legal obligations.

The army's documents show that recruiters target socio-economically vulnerable young people from age 16, particularly in families earning around £10,000 per year in deprived neighbourhoods. Three-quarters of 16-year-old recruits have a reading age of 11 or less (and seven percent have a reading age as low as five), precluding full comprehension of the legally binding enlistment papers. Recruiters are not required to meet with parents; a signature on a form, sent by post, and which recruiters have no means of verifying, is the only indication that parents understand and consent to their child's enlistment. In 2016 the UN criticised the UK's enlistment safeguards as 'insufficient' under international law.

Binding terms of service, high-risk roles

After an initial voluntary discharge window, enlisted minors are obliged from the day they turn 18 to remain in the army to the age of 22, having completed a minimum service period up to two years longer than is required for adult recruits. These legal obligations and the suspension of

certain fundamental rights that follow enlistment could not lawfully be imposed on civilian employees of any age.

The MoD wants the youngest recruits 'particularly for the infantry', where they are consequently overrepresented. The infantry faces the highest risks in war, suffering several times the rate of fatality found elsewhere in the armed forces and twice the prevalence of post-traumatic stress disorder (PTSD). Hence, although minors are not normally deployed to war zones, their disproportionate assignment to frontline combat roles leads to elevated risks over the course of their career. For example, soldiers who joined at age 16 and completed training were twice as likely to be killed in Afghanistan as those who enlisted as adults.

Mental health impact

Even before personnel may be deployed, a military setting carries unique risks that are incompatible with the legal right of minors to an environment conducive to their development. Prolonged stress, which is associated with basic soldier training, disproportionately affects young people in mid-adolescence, who are neuro-developmentally more vulnerable to it than adults, especially if they have had a stressful childhood.

According to research by King's College, armed forces personnel across all ranks and ages are twice as likely as civilians to suffer from anxiety and depression and 50 percent more likely to experience PTSD. These problems are more common among soldiers with combat roles, where enlisted minors are overrepresented. Among personnel who leave the forces within four years of joining – enlisted minors are again over represented in this group – 20 percent have screened positive for PTSD. Younger enlistees are most affected, being more likely than civilians of the same age and older enlistees to suffer from these stress-related mental health problems, and to drink heavily.

The army is sometimes thought to reduce antisocial behaviour among its youngest recruits, but the available evidence shows the opposite. A major study by King's College in 2013 found that military personnel across the age range were more likely than their civilian peers to commit violent, sexual, and drug-related offences. The study found that the rate of violent offending among enlistees actually increased after they joined up, and increased again after their first deployment, reaching twice the pre-enlistment rate.

Substandard education

All recruits are exempt from the provisions of the Education and Skills Act that set minimum standards for the duty to participate in education to the age of 18. The army's youngest recruits train at the Army Foundation College, which has been graded 'outstanding' by Ofsted under a specially designed inspection regime that focuses on welfare provision and excludes the standard of education from its scope. The government's recommended minimum educational attainment for the 16–19 age group is good passes in core GCSEs, which civilian colleges are required to offer as resits. They are not available in army training centres, which instead enrol 16-year-old recruits onto short, sub-GCSE courses in three subjects and an apprenticeship consisting of basic soldier training. The army's target for recruits' attainment after up to 12 months of military training is unambitious: Entry Level 3, which is equivalent to a reading age of 9–11.

Socioeconomic impact

It is sometimes suggested that young people from deprived backgrounds would be unemployed if they could not enlist until age 18. In fact, since four out of five of the most disadvantaged 16-year-olds now continue in full-time education, recruiting them for the army is less likely to rescue them from unemployment than to bring an early end to their full-time education. The practice leads to a high risk of unemployment, since 32 percent of soldiers who enlist as minors drop out of training; this would be considered unacceptable in a civilian college, where only nine percent of students in the same age group drop out.

It is also often suggested that the army helps disadvantaged young people to develop skills for later civilian employment, but the facts do not bear this out. Overall, veterans are no more likely than non-veterans to be in work and their jobs are more likely to be unskilled. The infantry has a particularly poor re-employment rate.

Unnecessary and expensive

A one-fifth reduction in the army's personnel requirement has brought transition to modern, all-adult armed forces within reach. As examined in detail elsewhere, the change would require only a small increase in adult intake, since a large proportion of those who now enlist as minors would still have done so as adults, had 18 been the minimum enlistment age. An all-adult army would benefit from soldiers who are more mature, less likely to leave during training, deployable immediately, and who do not need the duty of care arrangements required for younger personnel. The transition would also save money. It costs £53,000 to train an adult for the infantry, but £103,500 to train a minor for the same role to the same standard, for an army career that is only one-third longer on average.

Make it 18

Raising the enlistment age to 18 would put an end to the risks associated with joining the armed forces prematurely, while leaving open the option of a military career in adulthood. More 16-year-olds would stay in civilian education or training for longer to gain fundamental education and skills for lifelong employment.

The growing global consensus that only adults should be enlisted has already benefited countless children. While the British armed forces recruit from age 16 they lend legitimacy to other states and armed groups that still use children in armed conflict. In view of the UK's influence in the Commonwealth and UN Security Council, the transition to all-adult forces would be a major step towards a global end to child recruitment.

February 2019

www.child-soldiers.org

Women were kept out of infantry roles to make men more comfortable until today – that's shameful in itself

Why should it be women's responsibility to make themselves scarce because someday a man might fancy her a little too much and get distracted from the whopping great AK47 being shot at him?

By Harriet Hall

As of today, for the first time in history, all roles in the British military are open to women. That's over 2,000 years since Boadicea rode her horse-drawn chariot into battle against the Roman Empire; 871 years since Eleanor of Aquitaine led an army of 300 women to Jerusalem in the Second Crusade of 1147; 589 years since Joan of Arc cropped her hair, slipped on men's armour and led French troops to victory against the English at the besieged city of Orleans. That's not to mention Queen Cleopatra, the Greek Amazons and Margaret of Angou. I could go on.

In other words, women have been going to war for centuries – often winning. So why has it taken centuries for them to be formally able to serve in close combat on the front lines?

Announcing the news, the Ministry of Defence said that women currently serving in the Army are now able to transfer into infantry roles and those not presently serving will be able to apply to fight on the front lines from December, with new recruits training for the infantry and the Royal Marines to commence early 2019. Up until 2016, women were not permitted to serve in ground close combat roles at all.

Defence Secretary Gavin Williamson said that the changes 'are aimed at creating opportunities for individuals from all backgrounds and making the most of their talents. By making all branches and trades of the military open to everyone, regardless of their gender, the Armed Forces are building on their reputation of being a leading equal opportunities employer.' Hard to see how embracing gender equality today might allow you to 'build on' an existing reputation of excellence in equal opportunities; surely this is just the starting point. Nevertheless, any move away from gender-based discrimination is a positive move.

Naturally, the breaking of this seemingly sensible news has been met with the sort of social media response most feminists have become accustomed to dealing with. There's the age-old yawn-a-thon argument of women being 'Our mothers!' 'Our daughters!' 'Our sisters!' 'Our wives!' and therefore too weak or too precious to be allowed to get their hands dirty or their rifles out. It's always disheartening when women are qualified by their relationship to other people, as if we can only appreciate their abuse, loss or injury in those terms, rather than by simply thinking of them as human. But I digress.

The Twitterarti aren't the only people against this news. When David Cameron announced in 2016 that women would be allowed to perform combat roles, former SAS commander Colonel Tim Collins said that, 'The infantry is no place for a woman.' Calling the move 'politically correct extravagance', Collins said that bringing women into combat roles will 'drag our infantry to below the required standard' because they are 'physically weaker than men'. Of course, there's a very easy way round this: set one physical standard and allow any people – emphasis on people – who hit that standard to take up the job.

Army Chief Colonel Richard Kemp said that introducing women into close combat roles would be a move that would be 'paid for in blood', and would 'reduce the capability of the infantry, undermine our national defences and put lives in danger'. Exactly how that would come about remained unclear.

In 2002, then Defence Secretary, Geoff Hoon, said he was not prepared to lift the ban on women serving on the front line because officials were concerned that women's presence might distract men – either because of their innate need to protect women, or simply because of sexual attraction. A report into the matter, published in 2010 by Berkshire Consultancy and which the Ministry of Defence relied on for their position against including women, stated that: 'A significant number of men felt that, despite having had positive experiences of women, they would not want women in the infantry – there was a feeling amongst many that they would not feel comfortable asking a woman to close with and kill the enemy at very close range, and that

they were concerned about the woman's response to this situation arising. This final step is felt to be different and a step too far.'

Once again, women were being penalised because of male behaviours or sexual 'needs', and male assumptions about how they might act (no doubt based on tired, sexist stereotypes). Why should it be women's responsibility to make themselves scarce because someday a man might fancy her a little too much and get distracted from the whopping great AK47 being shot at him? Why should every woman in Britain be locked out of a job because a couple of men thought they might get hysterical in really tough situations?

It should go without saying that, to be able to serve in the infantry, women – just as men – will need to pass certain tests.

Despite suspicions from some social media conspiracists that these tests will now be made 'women friendly' with a dropped pass requirement, this has not been suggested by the Army at any point. As far as anyone can tell, that's just right-wing snowflake scare-mongering by people who would rather have their wives in the kitchen than in khakis.

The 2016 decision to include women in these roles – which will include carrying heavy supplies long distance and hand-to-hand combat – followed research by the Army that same year that suggested that of the 7,000 women then serving, just five percent would likely pass the infantry assessment. Now five percent isn't an enormous number, but at the time of the study, that amounted to 350 women – not exactly a small supply of additional soldiers, given that the Army appears to be desperately trying to increase enlistment with adverts in every cinema.

Williamson announced today that 'the military does not necessarily expect large numbers of women to apply for ground close combat roles', but that's not the point. The British Army concluded from the study that women would not have any effect whatsoever on a unit's ability to fight.

Female soldiers are just as worthy as their male counterparts – history has proved this to be true. And any physiological differences between the sexes should be utilised to create a more versatile army, not to block perfectly good soldiers from serving because they're invading male territory. The Australian military opened combat roles to women in 2011. Germany did it way before in 2001. And women in the US – a country which just allowed Brett Kavanaugh onto its Supreme Court – have been serving in frontline roles combat roles since 2013. That women are being allowed into these roles is not the thing we should be concerned about. If we should be angry about anything, it's how frankly shameful it is that it took us this long to get this far.

25 October 2018

I'm an army commanding officer, I've been to Afghanistan and Iraq and I've had two children

In brief

- ◆ **My first job was commanding a troop of all men**
- ◆ **I've been deployed to Iraq and Afghanistan and will go to South Sudan soon**
- ◆ **Doing a job I love sets an amazing example to my children**

Katie Hislop, 40, from Wiltshire, is the Commanding Officer of 32 Engineer Regiment in the British Army Royal Engineers. She joined the army 18 years ago and now lives on camp with her husband and two children.

Salary: At the start of officer training you will earn £25,984 and then 12 months later, on passing the training, that rises to £31,232.

People often ask me what it's like to be a woman in the army. The answer is that I've got no idea because I've always been in the army – ever since leaving university. I'm proud to be a woman in the army.

Commanding a regiment is something that I have aspired to throughout my career and I feel incredibly privileged to be in this role. It's a 24-7 job, but I love it.

I've been deployed to Kosovo, Iraq, Afghanistan and travelled across the world in my career.

Being sent to Iraq

In my first job in 2000, aged 22, I was in charge of a troop of 30 all-male soldiers in Germany. Women weren't allowed into the Royal Engineers as soldiers until 1998, so there weren't many women at that time.

I became an Adjutant, which is effectively a staff officer to the Commanding Officer. Then in 2005, I was deployed to Iraq for six months, where I was working all hours of the day, often through until midnight.

I really enjoyed my time in Iraq. There was a threat out there but it's what we spent so long training for.

My army family

I met my husband in the army and we have two girls together who are aged eight and ten. I took a year maternity leave to have my first child and then went back to work. I felt ready to go back. My husband worked full-time as well but we had good childcare and always shared the pick-ups and drop-offs between us.

We bought a house in a place fairly near to a lot of military bases just before we had our first daughter and lived there for ten years.

We were lucky – you only find out where you are going to get posted at the end of your two years in each job so you can't really make a ten-year plan. But we were able to work close enough to home to be able to share the childcare.

In 2013, I was deployed to Afghanistan. Professionally, going to Afghanistan was brilliant. At that stage, I was commanding a squadron of 120 people and we were exceptionally busy providing force protection across the whole of Helmand Province.

Leaving my children for five months was one of the hardest things I've ever done. My husband had transferred from the regular army to the reserve to give us a bit more flexibility so that he could have more time with the children while I was away.

Setting an example to my daughters

From a professional perspective, this was probably the most challenging and rewarding thing that somebody commanding a squadron could do. My husband and I decided we were happy for me to deploy. It was something I really wanted to do professionally and I think doing a job I love sets an amazing example to my children.

Our role in Afghanistan was to provide infrastructure support to all of the bases operating across Helmand. We also had to make sure the bases were well defended from Taliban attacks.

There is a period of adjustment when you arrive home after a deployment. You suddenly walk back into family life and it can take some time to get back to normal.

For some parents of very, very young children, some men and women can return from deployments to find their children feel they don't know them. We have a great welfare centre – most regiments do – who give advice on reintegrating with partners and children.

Moving house

My family and I now live on the camp I work at in Catterick, in North Yorkshire.

Moving to the camp was more of a change for my children as they had to move to a different school. That's something military children go through at least every two years in terms of finding a new school and making new friends.

Our girls have adapted very well to life on the camp. But if you continue to move around, the army will subsidise some of your boarding fees for keeping children in the same school.

There are quite a few couples who are parents and both in the military. Some are serving in the same area, some not, and all are juggling work and children between them.

For the last six months, I've been training to be deployed to South Sudan in July, as part of the United Nations mission out there. I'll be in charge of a task force of 400.

'Men and women can return from deployments to find their children feel they don't know them'. – Lt Col Katie Hislop

Our role out there will be to help build more accommodation blocks, better roads and better security in order that the United Nations military can then protect the civilians in South Sudan who are in desperate need of protection and food.

I was expecting to go to South Sudan – that is one of the reasons I asked for this job. It's a hugely interesting deployment and somewhere I have never been to before. Working with the UN means we will learn so much from the other nations who have been there for years.

You can have it all in the army

I want women to know that it is genuinely possible to have a career in the army and a family. There are lots of options as to where you can be posted and the timings of where you could work that mean you really can have both.

However, it's very important to make sure you have a network of support around you because it would be impossible for one person who is in the military to also have to do every single school run.

I feel really proud to be in the army, especially after recent events across the world. I think that we are valued and everywhere I go, particularly in the UK, people are always really positive when they find out what I do.

28 June 2018

Army diversity poster girl abused by fellow soldiers on social media

By Imogen Braddick

An army poster girl was abused by fellow soldiers on social media, it has emerged after the Ministry of Defence confirmed six soldiers had been disciplined for it.

The group of British troops based in Germany have been given formal warnings after posting racist remarks about Kerry-Ann Morris, the face of British Army Equality and Diversity campaigns.

The six soldiers from 159 (Colenso) Battery accused Cpl Morris of using her skin colour to secure promotions and 'playing the race card' at work to sabotage her colleagues' careers.

Comments were also made about Cpl Morris accusing others of being prejudiced against her because she is black, the *Mail on Sunday* reported.

Cpl Morris, from Nottingham, recently appeared in the 'Your Army Needs You' millennial recruitment campaign, which launched last month, and when the picture was circulated on Facebook, the group of soldiers based on Gutersloh posted a series of racist comments.

The comments reportedly received multiple 'likes' and the post was shared among other soldiers.

Cpl Morris, of Jamaican descent, is said to have brought it to the attention of the Army's Black, Asian and Minority Ethnic (BAME) Network – a group set up in 2017 for ethnic minority soldiers, of which Cpl Morris is a leading promoter.

A defence source told the newspaper that the soldiers who wrote and 'liked' the comments were interviewed by senior officers. They said: 'Cpl Morris is a high achiever and it appears some of her colleagues are looking for excuses as to why they're not doing as well as her. They know they will be in very serious trouble if they ever repeat such offensive accusations which breached the Army's values and standards policy.

'It was to Cpl Morris's credit that she requested the soldiers should be dealt with lightly on this occasion. As the victim, she could have pressed for more severe sanctions to be imposed but she was adamant that should not happen.'

An Army investigation concluded that the messages were racially abusive. The group faced being kicked out of the Army, but Cpl Morris reportedly intervened to persuade senior officers against severe punishment.

Cpl Morris joined the Army in 2011 and has been promoted twice – she recently transferred from the Royal Artillery to the Adjutant General's Corps. She has represented the Army and Combined Services at athletics and has appeared on the cover of the Army lifestyle magazine *The Locker*.

The latest recruitment drive that Cpl Morris features in was designed to focus on 'how the Army sees beyond stereotypes to spot young people's potential', the Ministry of Defence (MOD) said.

The Armed Forces has made other moves to address a deepening recruitment crisis, including allowing foreign nationals to join the Armed Forces without having ever lived in Britain - in the first quarter of 2018 only seven percent of the required number of soldiers had been recruited.

The campaign launched last month has reportedly led to a rise in the number of applications to join the Armed Forces.

The MOD has also set a target of 10 percent being from BAME backgrounds by 2020, with just 2.4 percent of personnel currently being from BAME communities.

For ranks below officer, 8.7 percent of all armed forces personnel were from ethnic minorities, but the MOD says the Army had the highest percentage of people from ethnic minorities working both as officers and in other ranks, compared with the other armed forces.

An MOD spokesman said: 'Discrimination and bullying have no place in the Armed Forces and will not be tolerated. All allegations are taken very seriously and are thoroughly investigated. Anyone found to have fallen short of our high standards can expect disciplinary action to be taken.'

17 February 2019

Navy one of UK's top LGBT-friendly employers

LGBT equality charity Stonewall has placed the naval service in 15th place on this year's Stonewall Workplace Equality Index, which lists the nation's top 100 organisations…

The Royal Navy was the first defence organisation to join Stonewall as a Diversity Champion in 2005 and has continued to support LGBT+ sailors and marines through its gender identity and sexual orientation network, Compass.

Second Sea Lord Vice Admiral Tony Radakin said: 'To fulfil our mission of keeping Britain safe, we rely on the skills of the most talented people regardless of their sexual orientation or gender identity. Not only do we want to reflect the communities we serve, but we know our people perform at their best when they can be themselves.

'Therefore we are fully committed to providing a workplace where our sailors and marines feel supported. I am immensely proud to see our continued efforts recognised with such a high position on the Stonewall Workplace Equality Index this year.'

Last year, the naval service enhanced its support of the LGBT+ community when Royal Marines officially took part in London Pride – their first time appearing at a Pride event. Sailors and marines were cheered on by hundreds of thousands of spectators as they were led through the capital by the Band of Her Majesty's Royal Marines from HMS Collingwood last July.

Commander Samantha Truelove, co-chair of the Compass Network, said: 'Growing our position in the Stonewall Workplace Equality Index is a ringing endorsement of who we are as an organisation. LGBT+ men and women should absolutely consider the Royal Navy or Royal Marines as a career option because we know our people are our strength.

'We will always provide a workplace where people can be themselves and differences are celebrated – it's your talent and commitment that matters. It feels great to be able to serve my country knowing my sexuality has no impact on the acceptance and support of my colleagues. I am proud to say I can truly be myself in the workplace and am valued for my contribution to the Royal Navy and wider defence.'

> _**'LGBT+ men and women should absolutely consider the Royal Navy or Royal Marines as a career option because we know our people are our strength.'**_
>
> _**– Commander Samantha Truelove**_

21 January 2019

www.pathfinderinternational.co.uk

Armed forces workforce

Main facts and figures

- As at October 2018, people from ethnic minorities (not including White minorities) made up 2.5% of officers in the UK regular armed forces, compared with 2.4% in April 2012

- For ranks below officer, 8.8% of all armed forces personnel were from ethnic minorities, compared with 7.9% in April 2012

- The Army had the highest percentage of people from ethnic minorities working both as officers and in other ranks, compared with the other armed forces

By ethnicity, service and rank

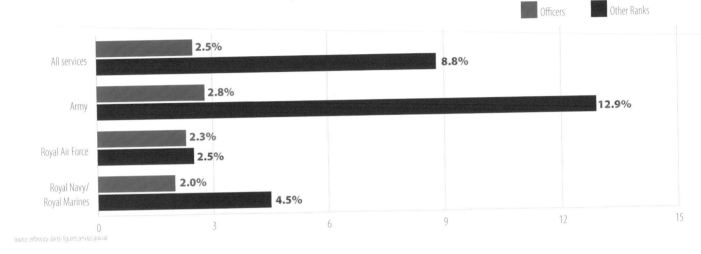

Percentage of armed forces personnel from ethnic minorities (excluding White minorities) by service and rank

Source: ethnicity-facts-figures.service.gov.uk

Summary

This data shows that:

- Overall, people from ethnic minorities (not including White minorities) made up 2.5% of officers in the UK armed forces and 8.8% of other ranks as at October 2018

- People from ethnic minorities made up 2.8% of officers in the Army, compared with 2.3% of those in the Royal Air Force, and 2.0% of those in the Royal Navy/Royal Marines

- Among personnel in other ranks, people from ethnic minorities made up 12.9% of those in the Army, 4.5% of those in the Royal Navy/Royal Marines, and 2.5% of those in the Royal Air Force

By ethnicity and service over time (officers only)

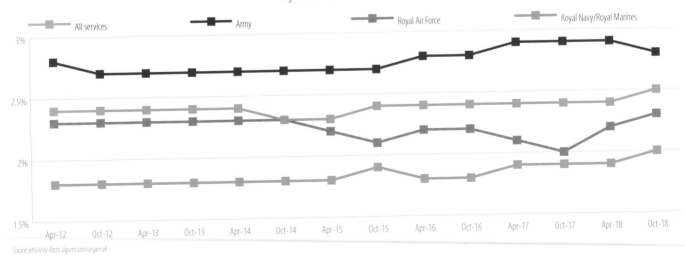

Percentage of armed forces officers from ethnic minorities (not including White minorities), by service over time

Source: ethnicity-facts-figures.service.gov.uk

Summary

This data shows that:

◆ Overall, between April 2012 and October 2018, the percentage of officers from ethnic minorities (not including White minorities) in the UK armed forces rose slightly, from 2.4% to 2.5%

◆ In the Army, the percentage of officers from ethnic minorities remained relatively stable, at 2.8% in both April 2012 and October 2018

◆ In the Royal Air Force, the percentage of officers from ethnic minorities remained constant at 2.3%

◆ In the Royal Navy/Royal Marines, the percentage of officers from ethnic minorities increased from 1.8% to 2.0%

By ethnicity and service over time (non-officer ranks only)

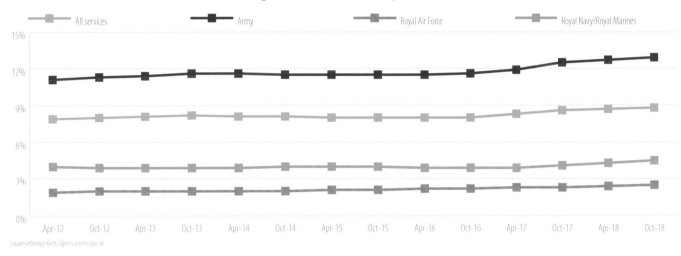

Percentage of armed forces personnel in non-officer ranks from ethnic minorities (not including White minorities), by service over time

Source: ethnicity-facts-figures.service.gov.uk

Summary

This data shows that:

◆ Between April 2012 and October 2018, the percentage of UK armed forces personnel in non-officer ranks who were from ethnic minorities (other than White minorities) increased from 7.9% to 8.8%

◆ Of all the armed forces, the Royal Air Force has consistently had the lowest percentage of personnel from ethnic minorities in non-officer ranks, despite an increase from 1.9% in April 2012 to 2.5% in October 2018

◆ The Army had the largest increase in the percentage of people from ethnic minorities in non-officer ranks, from 11.1% in April 2012 to 12.9% in October 2018

◆ The percentage of people from ethnic minorities in non-officer ranks in the Royal Navy/Royal Marines remained between 3.9% and 4.5% over the period shown

12 June 2019

Things you need to know

The data is taken from human resources records by the Ministry of Defence on 1 April and 1 October every year.

The lower representation of certain ethnic minorities in the armed forces could in part be explained by eligibility criteria for joining, including nationality, security and health. For example, migrants to the UK won't be able to join the armed forces unless they have:
• the right to remain indefinitely in the UK
• lived in the UK for more than five years if they are from a Commonwealth country.

Since 2009, Gurkha personnel have been able to transfer into the Army. This may partially explain the larger proportion of people from ethnic minorities in the Army compared with the other armed forces.

These statistics relate to people whose ethnicity was declared. At 1 October 2018, the percentage of personnel in the UK regular armed forces who declared an ethnicity was 99%.

For this data, the number of armed forces personnel was too small to draw any firm conclusions about specific or broad ethnic categories. Therefore, the data is broken down into the following two broad categories:
•White – White ethnic groups (including White British and White ethnic minorities)
•Other – all other ethnic minorities.

www.gov.uk

Out of conflict, out of mind

This Armed Forces Day, SSAFA calls on the nation to update their view of the Forces and celebrate the 'everyday' heroes serving our country...

New research from SSAFA, the Armed Forces charity, reveals outdated misconceptions of the modern-day military are having a concerning impact on public support for the Forces. The findings, commissioned for Armed Forces Day, show over a third of the UK do not actively support the Armed Forces, rising to 48% for those aged 16–34.

Concerningly, 43% would only support an Armed Forces charity during times of conflict and one in five admit they would never support a military charity. This lack of support seems to be linked to a widespread lack of awareness of who the Forces are and what they do. Despite the UK's military not being in active conflict for almost five years:

- 52% are more familiar with the roles of the Armed Forces while engaged in active conflict, than they are now

- 50% of the public are unaware of where our Forces are based in the world, with 16% mistakenly believing the majority to still be in Afghanistan

- 58% know more about historical military events, such as D-Day, than they do about our current military.

Two-thirds of those surveyed admit, when thinking of the Armed Forces, they stereotypically picture a frontline, camouflage-clad soldier or a fighter pilot. However, this is far from reality, with the modern military having a vast infrastructure including logistics, healthcare and education, as well as national defence.

Surgeon Lieutenant Commander, Elizabeth James, a doctor for over ten years in the Royal Navy, said: 'I've found myself facing questions about why we need doctors in the military when we aren't in active conflict – but people forget that there are over 190,000 people in the military at any given time, as well as their families. The Navy and other Forces are permanently deploying all over the world, both on land in support of UN missions and at sea.

'They rely on good medical care, and ready support for when we are back in conflict, and that's what the medical and nursing services are there for. It's wonderful to be celebrated during Armed Forces Week, but to be understood and appreciated all year round would mean even more. That way, we would feel confident that we have the support of the public whilst we work to protect our country.'

Worryingly, a lack of knowledge surrounding the Armed Forces' role in society today, is directly impacting military charities like SSAFA. Keen for this to change is Sir Andrew Gregory, CEO of SSAFA, who said: 'SSAFA is very proud to be the official charity partner of Armed Forces Day 2019; the event allows us to thank those who serve our country in the Royal Navy, Royal Marines, British Army and Royal Air Force.

'Our Armed Forces, along with their families, make sacrifices on a daily basis to protect our way of life and the freedoms we cherish, something that should never be forgotten. As I write there are many military operations currently underway and thousands of troops stationed overseas. Armed Forces Day is an opportunity for the nation to remember that, even when they are not headline news, our Armed Forces are working tirelessly on our behalf.

'Take a moment this week to appreciate the liberties and democracy we enjoy in our country; that is what those individuals are protecting. And when those who are serving or have served in this nation's Armed Forces, and their families, need emotional, practical or financial support, SSAFA is there to assist them – as we have done for the last 135 years.'

26 June 2019

The above information is reprinted with kind permission from Pathfinder International.
© 2019 Baltic Publications

www.pathfinderinternational.co.uk

UK armed forces mental health

Adjustment Disorders
30%

PTSD
6%

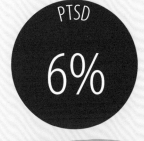

Other Neurotic Disorders
28%

Other Mental Disorders
2%

Mood Disorders
32%

Psychoactive Substance Misuse
4%

Mental Disorders

3.1%

of UK Armed Forces personnel were assessed with a mental disorder at MOD Specialist Mental Heath Services in 2017–18

6.1%
of females

2.7%
of males

2.9%	**2.2%**	**2.9%**	**2.9%**
of Royal Navy	of Royal Marines	of Army	of RAF

My life after post-traumatic stress disorder (PTSD)

To mark Mental Health Awareness Week, a veteran with post-traumatic stress disorder (PTSD) reflects on the care provided by the NHS Veterans' Clinic in London, also known as the Veterans' Mental Health Transition, Intervention and Liaison Service (TILS).

I left the Parachute Regiment with an injury and, unknown to me, PTSD.

By my 19th birthday I had served in combat tours, but civvy street was proving to be the toughest challenge. My spinal injury I understood and dealt with it in Military 'P' company fashion; get it sorted. I exercised diligently but ignored the raging mind-frag.

They had not coined the term PTSD when I left, so most of my adult life was spent tossed this way and that by what I thought was my own madness. I flitted from job to job, country to country, menial work and labouring. Urgent desire to keep travelling, keep one step ahead, running from the unrecognised effect of trauma.

Periods of hyper-alertness and manic activity spiralled into an exhausted well of depression. I'd cut myself away and struggled to fight my way back to the surface, until I felt able to emerge and carry on. Long solo road trips, hiking and camping, far away from people.

Years of wasted relationships, closing myself off from those close to me, fearing that they would see what I felt. A sense of low self-esteem would wash over me like a tide of despair, if I stood still too long. Keep moving and finding missions, self-medicate when it gets out of control. That was my instinctive response.

It was years before I got help: I'd turned 60 and was begging my GP for super strong sleeping pills; flashbacks were keeping me awake. I felt very low. The GP sent me to the St Pancras Hospital Veterans Clinic (the Veterans' Mental Health Transition, Intervention and Liaison Service).

Like many before me, I had the panic attack. They'll find that stuff buried in my mind! Memories I had pushed away, a dark disturbing box of images, constantly fluttering subconsciously, a shark threatening to surface. I spent ages in the toilet shaking like a leaf, then pulled myself together and pressed the buzzer for the Veterans Clinic. I was welcomed by a friendly face.

The Veterans Clinic was a revelation. An hour and, several glasses of water and a couple of sniffs of lavender oil later, they explained what I was going through. My symptoms had over the years got a deep hold and would not release their debilitating grip, unless I did something about it and was ready to process my memories. Mission on.

Importantly, I came to understand that they were just symptoms. Over the year of therapy, I began to understand that they were an automatic response system to trauma of months of alertness, switched on for combat. A teenager's brain has not yet fully formed and these symptoms are driven deep, creating their own neural pathways.

I remember coming out of an intense therapy session, feeling light and as if I floated back home – everything seemed insubstantial, unreal. The therapist had cautioned me to go home and take time out. I sat in my kitchen brewed some coffee and memories bubbled up, all connected to the trauma we had processed that day. These were important memories, buried alongside the twitching, disturbing itch of combat memories. I hurriedly jotted down notes, not wanting these memories to fade.

Coming to terms with PTSD was a liberating experience; I began to audit my life, small steps, to understand many of my mistakes and weird responses to life's journey. My uneasiness in crowds and my temper and simmering anger, which would bubble up for no reason, all triggered subconsciously. But now I had context and could talk to my teenage soldier self; understanding flowed and the world lost its hidden threats.

After therapy I started writing, I couldn't stop. Making up for lost time, I not only finished my book, but got it published. *Falling Soldiers*, published by Brigand, is a fictional novel that allowed me to explore injury and PTSD through the safety valve of narrative. It allowed me to take a safe step away, whilst still tackling the memories. My characters had left the army, but they felt lost overboard at sea, grabbing onto anything, which would keep them afloat. Examining how they survived in civvy street wasn't a confession, but it was close enough.

I joined the Soldiers Arts Academy, met other veterans, banter broke out and we dealt with our similar issues collectively. I wrote and performed at the Shakespeare's Globe on Remembrance Sunday, 'Soldiers salute to Shakespeare'. The angst moved over and made way for creativity. Life became a kaleidoscope of rainbow coloured experiences to be enjoyed and savoured.

So now I'm writing, acting and healing with NWLive, a group of Veterans developing a play on life after PTSD, performed at Kentish Town medical centre.

And I will always offer my heartfelt thanks to the NHS mental health services at the St Pancras Veterans Clinic.

13 May 2019

We need to talk about suicide in the military

An article from The Conversation.

THE CONVERSATION

By Simon Harold Walker, Associate Researcher, University of Strathclyde

In 1916, a young British private in northern France wrote home to his parents explaining his decision to take his own life. A survivor of the early days of the Somme, considered one of the most brutal battles of World War I, Robert Andrew Purvis apologised to his family before praising his commanding officers and offering the remainder of his possessions to his comrades. Purvis's surviving suicide note remains one of the only documents of its kind from World War I.

Our research into suicide during World War I has shown that it was not uncommon – although reporting of it was rare. For the armed forces, recognition and support for these cases has been a long-standing struggle. From 1923, the Scottish charter for the honour roll of the fallen explicitly forbade the inclusion of suicide cases, which meant that reported cases from World War II were also omitted from the honour roll in the Scottish National War Museum at Edinburgh Castle.

An 'illness'

At the turn of the 20th century, suicide was often regarded as a symptom of mental illness. Cases of suicide, if recorded at all, were almost always marked as being a case of 'temporary insanity'. Britain stood at the forefront of treatment for conflict-related mental illness as the Craiglockhart War Hospital in Edinburgh became famous for treating shell-shocked soldiers.

The hospital evolved to advance the fledgling understanding of conflict-related psychosis and specialised in practical recovery techniques including sports, model-making, writing, photography and the 'talking cure' pioneered by psychologist William Rivers.

Craiglockhart is also known for treating famous patients, including war poets Siegfried Sassoon and Wilfred Owen. Sassoon remains the only recognised war poet to have published on the controversial topic of soldier suicide.

Haunted men

Due to the stigma, controversy and inflammatory nature of the topic, discussions surrounding mental health and suicide in the British military were limited for much of the 20th century. Victor Gregg, a serviceman in World War II, recounted in an interview in 2015 how psychological aftercare for demobilised men in 1945 was non-existent, lamenting:

My brain was filled with images of suffering that were to haunt me for the next 40 years… The final gift from a grateful country was a civilian suit, a train ticket home and about £100 of back-service pay.

Sixty-four years later, fortunately much has changed. At the turn of the 21st century, both the military and governments in the UK have come to recognise the issue of military-related suicide.

But despite the increase in mental health awareness and support campaigns for both serving soldiers and veterans over the past two decades, concerns over deaths continue. The Ministry of Defence spends £22 million a year on mental healthcare for veterans, with a further £6 million annually for support within the NHS. But military charities argue that this is not enough – particularly as focused statistical recording and analysis of veteran suicide cases only began in earnest after 2001.

In March 2019, Scottish warrant officer Robert McAvoy, a veteran of 20 years' service, took his own life. The following month 18-year-old Highlander Alistair McLeish died by suicide at Catterick Garrison in York. These tragedies are by no means unique.

In 2018, research by a Scottish newspaper demonstrated that a former member of the forces takes their own life in Scotland every six days. This prompted the Scottish mental health minister Clare Haughey to publicly pledge closer consideration of the mental healthcare of Scottish soldiers and veterans.

Concerns over the suicides of 71 British veterans and serving personnel in 2018 led UK defence secretary, Tobias Ellwood, to tell *ITV News*:

I'm truly sorry. I'm sorry that they feel the armed forces, NHS, government, have let them down.

This was not an admission of responsibility for a lack of duty of care. It was a poor excuse for an apology which undercut the severity of the issue and role of the establishment within it, by insinuating that the 'lack of support given' was a matter of perception. However, Ellwood also admitted: 'We must improve.'

Addressing the issues

Suicide is currently the biggest killer of men under the age of 45 in the Western world – and the concerns of suicide related to service are not limited to Britain.

In the US, 6,000 veterans took their own lives in 2018, on top of the suicides of 275 active service personnel. In the American media and public eye, service and veteran suicide is perceived as a growing issue as cases of mental illness and post-traumatic stress continue to go untreated.

Military service and veteran suicide are not new issues, but there are crucial conversations to be had about the subject publicly, politically, socially and medically. Claiming there is a suicide 'epidemic' would be an exaggeration as the numbers do not support that kind of term, but the issue remains pertinent and in need of public attention.

Bluntly, men and women have died, are dying and will continue to die if society does not examine the issue of military suicide. Only through open discussion, active research and recognition of service and veteran mental health-related deaths can these tragedies be prevented in the future.

The veterans' mental health charity Combat Stress is available 24 hours on 0800 138 1619 for veterans and their families; 0800 323 444 for serving personnel and their families; via text on 07537 404719; or at www.combatstress.org.uk

28 June 2019

Doing battle: how the military is helping tackle mental health problems

Veteran John Mayhead on overcoming PTSD and highlighting the complexities of dealing with military mental health problems.

Strangely, it wasn't the obvious trauma that most affected me. The horrors of war – luck separating the unscathed and the maimed, dead friends, wounded children – these are the awful reality of combat but one that my Army training had prepared me for since the day, aged 19, I had joined.

No, it was the other, more insidious trauma that caught me out. Like a bully who waits to pounce when you're least expecting it, I found myself blind-sided by other stuff: month after month of deploying on immediate 'notice to move' – Army parlance for having to react without warning or preparation to any incident. If something went bang in the northern half of Basra in the summer of 2005, I was the person in command of the incident. And, in the midst of what was effectively a civil war, there were lots of bangs.

Ironically, it was a fight I thought I had won. Through exceptional hard work, huge amounts of professionalism by them and more than a little luck, my company of 105 soldiers had all survived the tour. As infantry soldiers in that environment, when we'd dealt daily with bombs, rocket attacks and shootings with scores of other casualties, it was an almost miraculous statistic. Sure, there was a fair amount of emotion that came out of me once we'd returned to the UK, but I dealt with that in the way soldiers have for thousands of years: I got drunk with the people I had shared the experience with. After a couple of months, I thought that was it.

But that wasn't it. Anger was the first symptom. Pure, unadulterated rage flowed out of me. It was triggered by the innocuous: a printer playing up; someone cutting me up in their car; even somebody stepping out in front on me on a busy pavement. At home, the rage sometimes spilled over; one afternoon I let out my anger on a chair, smashing it to pieces in my spare bedroom. Sleep became difficult – at night the demons came out to play, and as a result I came to fear the darkness.

Other self-destructive actions followed: I remember driving down dark country roads, taking my hands off the wheel, closing my eyes and pushing my foot on the accelerator pedal. At that point it wasn't suicide I longed for, just to tempt fate; almost to see if survival in Iraq meant something. I also found myself yearning for revenge against the faceless enemy who had killed and maimed so many. I applied for another tour in Afghanistan, keen to fight again, this time with the gloves off. Fortunately, the application was denied.

Finally, in the summer of 2006, my family convinced me I needed help. Ironically, I'd been advising many of my soldiers to seek medical advice for mental injuries, but shied away from it myself. I was worried about the stigma attached to mental health problems and, in a term that would come to haunt me, felt as a commander I 'should' be able to cope. I was given three one-hour therapy sessions with an Army psychiatrist, put a sticking plaster over the gaping wound in my head, and once again thought I was better.

I wasn't. Over the next few years I went from stratospheric highs to self-destructive lows. After another short tour in Afghanistan in 2009 I left the Army, but that didn't solve anything. Now on anti-depressants, I lost my job, house, and a friend to cancer within a two-week period. Even my dog dropped dead; the world seemed stacked against me, and as a result I ceased to function. I've always wondered what people meant by 'having a breakdown'; I now know.

With two tiny kids, my wife carried me and I came to rely on her totally. We found a new place to live and started again. Still afraid deep-down of the stigma of seeking NHS help, I paid for private counselling. It helped, a bit. I found a job as a writer, doing something I have always loved, and helped facilitate a programme for Help for Heroes. I felt my experience was helping others, and for a while all was good. I didn't realise at the time, but although I was helping other veterans, I was also taking on some of their burden and from time to time I found myself unable to cope. Anxiety and depression took over. With Help for Heroes' support, I had counselling and started a course of cognitive behavioural therapy (CBT) with my local NHS mental health team. Again it helped, but again it was temporary.

The big change in my life came in 2017. Last summer, the pressures of work, life and what was finally formally diagnosed as PTSD, combined to tip me over the edge. My lowest ebb was sitting in a lay-by, unable to reach a friend

who had until then been my lifeline. I didn't want to kill myself, but didn't want to put my family through any more pain. I rang the Samaritans. The guy on the other end of the line did what that wonderful charity does best: listened with a sympathetic ear. After a while I felt strong enough to go home.

A few days later we went to stay with a friend. He's been through a huge amount of trauma, both in the Army and in his personal life, and he gave me a book that fundamentally changed me: *Go Wild!* by Dr John Ratey and Richard Manning. It made me, for the first time, consider all the elements together: mental and physical health, diet, the importance of family and friends. I finished the book in a day, and decided to change what I could. I stopped eating refined sugar, or as much as that is possible these days. I cut back my carbohydrate intake to those in fresh vegetables and fruit. I then put on my trainers, and in the middle of a rainstorm, went for my first run in months.

A couple of weeks later, my wife told me about a documentary she had seen on the power of cold water immersion to help people with depression. I searched for it and stumbled upon a University of Portsmouth team who are researching just this, and who hold weekly sea swims. In early January, with the sea a balmy six degrees Celsius, I took my first dip. I still try to swim weekly, and cold shower every day. In a few weeks I'm running my first trail marathon in 17 years and have entered an ultra marathon in October. I'm about 15 kilos lighter than I was in October last year, and feeling great.

I now see my diet, running and cold water immersion as my three 'meds'. I take them daily and will do for the rest of my life. I'm not taking away the amazing professional support I've had, but I know that these things are within my own power: it gives me an edge over the mental health bully.

By March 2018, with my moods much more stable, my mental and physical health much improved, I received word of the Walk Of America run by the charity Walking With The Wounded, who help vulnerable ex-service personnel. I needed a challenge to test myself, went for an interview, and was duly offered a place. At the beginning of June, I will fly with the team to LA, then spend two weeks walking a couple of hundred miles through California and Texas. I'll then leave the core team to continue on. Six wounded ex-service people from the UK and US are walking more than 1,000 miles over a 14-week period, with the aim of highlighting the complexities of dealing with military mental health problems.

And, as the charity's patron, Prince Harry, recently said, it is a complex problem. One of the issues I wrote about earlier, the feeling that you 'should' be able to cope, is one of the biggest stumbling blocks. It stops so many people coming forward and seeking help, or delays their recovery. If I had been shot in Iraq, I wouldn't have considered trying to deal with that injury myself. The sooner we see mental health problems as wounds that need professional help to deal with, then the sooner people will get treatment.

Since I've started talking about my own journey, I've been amazed by the other people who have admitted they have had similar problems, or that they've lived it through their brothers, partners or friends. From my own experiences, I've seen that these are illnesses that can develop and grow over many years, only coming to a head sometimes decades after the person has left the Armed Forces. Charities such as Walking With The Wounded and Help for Heroes do an amazing job in supporting those people, but without daily news reports of physical casualties from the war zone, they have dropped in people's consciousness and are not as financially well-supported as in previous years. Hopefully, by our Walk Of America (with a little help from our royal patron) we can change that.

25 May 2018

Alcohol misuse is more common in the armed forces than post-traumatic stress disorder

An article from The Conversation

THE CONVERSATION

By Daniel Leightley, Postdoctoral Research Associate, King's College London, Jo-Anne Puddephatt, PhD candidate in the Addictions Research Group, University of Liverpool, Laura Goodwin, Senior Lecturer in Epidemiology of Mental Health and Addiction, University of Liverpool, and Nicola Fear, Director of the King's Centre for Military.

Alcohol has historically been used in the UK armed forces to encourage bonding and to deal with difficult experiences. And while alcohol use is now on the decline, harmful drinking in the forces is still double that of the general population.

To put this into perspective, about 11% of men and 5% of women in the UK armed forces meet the criteria for alcohol misuse. This means they are drinking at a level that is likely to be harmful to their health.

Compare this with about 4% of men and 2% of women in the general population. Yet many of those drinking at a harmful level in the armed forces do not recognise they have a problem.

A common problem

People serving in the forces drink alcohol for a range of reasons – for pleasure, due to social pressures and to cope with either day-to-day stresses or with mental health symptoms. Mental health problems are more common in the armed forces so it's maybe not surprising that alcohol is often used to cope.

The consequences of excessive alcohol consumption are wide reaching and can directly impact families of servicemen or women. And research has also shown that when people leave the armed forces – and the drinking culture – their alcohol consumption does not decrease.

Alcohol misuse is more common in the armed forces than post-traumatic stress disorder, yet it receives much less attention. Within this community, only around a third of those who self report an alcohol problem say they've sought help. This means that the large majority of those who need to reduce their drinking are not doing so.

Problem drinking

It's understandable that the stigma of being labelled 'an alcoholic' may put people off going to get help. But there's also the issue that many of those who would benefit from decreasing their alcohol use don't actually meet the criteria for an alcohol use disorder. This is despite the fact that they may be drinking above the recommended guidelines. This is important given recent findings show that even moderate levels of drinking have negative health consequences.

Our preliminary research has found that many people who are worried about their drinking, or who want to keep a track on how much they are consuming, turn to alcohol apps to help monitor and keep on top of the problem. Popular apps include Drink Less, Drink Aware and Drink Free Days which encourage users to regularly record and monitor (via visual graphics) their alcohol consumption.

And there is clearly a value to this technology, given research suggests these types of apps can be at least as effective as face-to-face brief interventions for alcohol.

The research

Our project, a collaboration between King's Centre for Military Health Research and University of Liverpool, funded by the Medical Research Council, aimed to find out if an app could also support people in the armed forces to reduce their drinking.

We developed an app, to help people monitor and manage their alcohol consumption. The app allows users to set goals, and compare their drinking to civilians and others in the armed forces' community.

The algorithms can also autonomously detect changes in behaviour and provide real-time support to the patient – while in parallel could be used to alert healthcare professionals to enable intervention.

To test the app, we ran a four-week study with 31 people in the armed forces who drank at hazardous levels. Our initial findings suggest the app could be useful to help people tackle problems of alcohol misuse.

In our study, we found that participants opened the app on average 29 times during the four-week period. All participants used the drink diary function of the app to monitor their alcohol use across the study period. At the start of the study. participants consumed a median of 5.6 units per drinking day, which decreased to 4.7 units by the last week.

Though our study did highlight that despite using the app, many of the participants drinking heavily still didn't feel they had a problem. This may explain why some features of the app such as 'goal setting' were not used as much as the drinks diary.

The right support

Research has shown that people who are drinking too much ultimately need support to understand more about their own drinking behaviours and how they can cut down – and we hope that our app can help to provide this.

We now hope to further refine the app taking on board feedback received during our feasibility study, culminating in a public release later this year.

So given that harmful drinking in the armed forces is substantially higher compared to the general population and that research has shown how effective digital technologies can be as a health intervention, it is hoped that our app could have the potential to tackle the problem culture of drinking in the UK armed forces.

2 April 2019

After I was hit by a grenade, my biggest concerns were for my family

By Nick Garland

In early 2008, as a young officer, I was set to deploy to Afghanistan. It was the culmination of a year and a half of intense training and I was primed to go.

For my family and friends, it was a stressful period of limbo as they waited for me to fly and were reminded of where I was going by the almost daily casualty reports. For me it was a long-awaited adventure. Ten weeks into the tour my adventure became my family's nightmare when I was seriously injured by a rocket-propelled grenade.

My injuries were life-threatening and I was not well, but kept unconscious in an induced coma, I was not suffering. For my family and those close to me, however, their suffering had just begun. It started with a knock on the door – a moment that is never forgotten – by two soldiers charged with the thankless task of informing my family that their life had changed irreversibly.

When telling my story, I always mention the victims. The people that were there, that I shared my blood with; the pilots that flew to pick me up when they were out of fuel, the surgeons and doctors that trialled new things to keep me here. And of course my family who endured the stress of surgery and the bedside helplessness that was a blur to me, if I even remembered at all.

It is these people that bear invisible scars and memories, it is these people that we, the trauma survivors, owe our lives to. While I am healthy, their journey continues. For them, merely watching a film can spark memories of a dark time that I can never share with them.

As I root for our Invictus Games gladiators this week I will be thinking most of the families watching and the trauma they undoubtedly still battle with every day. Secondary trauma is little known and rarely understood, but it is significant, long-lasting and almost always forgotten.

My wife, family and friends are victims of my injury. They were exposed to the graphic reality of combat medicine and this became their world while I was barely part of it.

My family are far from unique in this. Nearly a decade on from the worst years of the British Afghan mission, there are hundreds, if not thousands of others across the country, quietly supporting their husbands or wives, brothers and sisters, girlfriends, boyfriends, daughters and sons.

For some it is physical trauma. For some it is not. But it is a shared trauma. There has never been such a pivotal time for the service family to be exactly that, a family.

This week the Royal British Legion supported the families of wounded and injured servicemen and women by sending them to Toronto to watch their athletes compete in the third Invictus Games. This is just one example of the Legion's little known work to care for the families of veterans, but one that is crucial on the road to recovery for families that have been through so much.

This road is a long one, unseen and unmentioned. My trauma journey is over; it was done in a few short seconds, and then a long sleep in a hospital bed. For the others, their trauma lives on.

Major Nick Garland is with 1st The Queen's Dragoon Guards.

26 September 2017

Commonwealth veterans face UK visa fees and deportation

British Legion says treatment of ex-soldiers is 'a poor way to say thank-you'.

By Caroline Davies

Hundreds of Commonwealth military veterans who risked their lives serving in the UK armed forces face spiralling debts after being forced to pay 'exorbitant' visa fees to remain in the country after their discharge, campaigners have said.

Before Commonwealth Day on Monday, the Royal British Legion is calling on the government to scrap the fees as a matter of urgency, saying it is scant thanks for veterans.

The fees for indefinite leave to remain have risen by 127% in five years to £2,389 per person, amounting to almost £10,000 for a family of four. Since their introduction in 2003, the fees have risen by 1,441%. If veterans cannot pay, or their application fails, they can face deportation.

The charity said the government must address the issue as a matter of urgency as the Ministry of Defence aims to increase recruitment from Commonwealth countries – mainly in Africa, the Caribbean, and from Fiji – to 1,300 a year.

Many face desperate financial problems on discharge, sometimes paying the fees on credit cards, but as they are unable to work or claim benefits while their applications are processed, amass huge debts, the charity said. In a letter to the immigration minister, Caroline Nokes, it calls on the government to grant a waiver of fees in the next parliamentary session and abolish the fees altogether after that.

'These Commonwealth veterans are facing a desperate situation,' said Charles Byrne, director general of the Royal British Legion. 'They have left their homeland and given years of loyal service to the United Kingdom. They should be able to continue living in the UK with their families without incurring significant financial costs.

'This is a poor way of saying thank-you to people we encouraged to leave their countries to come and serve in the British armed forces. As Commonwealth Day approaches, we urge the home secretary to take action to help Commonwealth military veterans… and abolish all visa application fees.'

Each year, around 500 Commonwealth personnel leave the armed forces and are faced with these costs, or the possibility of deportation. In 2017, around 7.1% of army recruits were from Commonwealth countries. While serving, they are exempt from UK immigration controls, but exemption is removed upon discharge. Those who have served more than four years are eligible to apply for indefinite leave to remain.

The British Legion is asking people to support the campaign by writing to their MP. Previous successful campaigns have focused on the settlement rights of Gurkhas and Afghan interpreters who supported UK troops in Afghanistan.

Andy Pike, the Legion's public policy manager, said: 'If you are going to ask somebody to come here, risk their lives in service to this country, and everything else we ask of our armed forces, it's only fair we allow them to stay. These are Commonwealth veterans who have done their time, who have served, and whom the nation owes a debt of gratitude to.'

'I couldn't work. I was sleeping in my car'

Paul, 27, came from Nigeria to the UK to study, but joined the Royal Logistics Corps after recruiters visited his university, erroneously believing that the army would pay for him to return to his studies after he had served. But on army exercises in Canada he contracted non-freezing cold injury, causing severe nerve damage to his hands and feet, and was medically discharged in 2017 after serving three years and eight months.

A father to UK-born twins, but separated from their mother, he was just short of the four years required to apply for residency, so had to apply first for limited leave to remain, and then again for indefinite leave to remain. It took more than two months to process his first application.

Paul, now studying law in the UK, said: 'I wasn't able to register with a GP, or get any help from the local authorities. I couldn't work. I was sleeping in my car.

'It was hard, hard, hard. Because of my medical condition, I needed to have warm clothes on all the time, but all the ones that were issued to me during my service, I had to return after I left. So I was running my car with the heater on. My car was my home.

'I was struggling to feed myself. I would go two or three days without eating proper food, or anything at all. I was depending on family back home to send me money just to feed myself.'

He thought about returning to Nigeria, but that would mean never seeing his young twins. 'I wanted to be part of their lives, and I didn't want to go back home and never be able to see them.'

He paid the first set of fees out of his army lump sum, but had no money to pay the second, and turned to the British Legion for financial help. 'I was desperate. I had two options: to make the application, or not to be part of my children's upbringing. Without the British Legion, I would probably be somewhere in Nigeria, but not being able to see my children, my life would not be worth living any more.'

With the charity's help, he was eventually granted indefinite leave to remain, but he feels unfairly treated by the Home Office following his military service for the UK.

'I didn't get any thanks for it. If I had stayed a student, I would have remained on a student visa, pending a Home Office decision. But when you are a Commonwealth soldier, as soon as you leave the military, you have no rights, no thanks. It's horrible.'

8 March 2019

Military partners need empathy – not pity

An article from The Conversation

THE CONVERSATION

By Emma Long, PhD Candidate Sociology/Social Work, Lancaster University

Partners of people in the armed forces can feel alienated by stereotypical ideas and notions about what it is like to serve in the military. The 'he/she knew what they were signing up for' response is all too common. My research looked at what British army partners go through when spouses return from deployment. It has revealed they often feel misunderstood, uncomfortable and frustrated in non-military company.

Due to changes being made to the military family housing model and personal drives to protect the family from regular relocations, army families are now more likely to be living away from bases and alongside civilians. Therefore, the public needs to be educated about the realities of military life – for soldiers and partners alike.

The current model of the military community is built around the military base. Personnel can live on or near to their duty station, with their families, in Service Families Accommodation. By living in close proximity, military families develop deep connections with one another. However, the proportion of army families living in this type of accommodation during the working week has decreased from 76% in 2010 to 68% in 2017.

Generally, army families choose to live away from bases to protect the career and education of non-serving members from relocations (army families move every two to three years) and to live close to the wider family. Additionally, the introduction of the Future Accommodation Model over the coming years will likely lead to more families living off-base, alongside civilians. The model aims to increase the variety of accommodation by offering military families financial subsidies to rent in the private sector.

However, my research has found that army partners often feel misunderstood by the civilian community. Separation from a community that understands and immersion into a community that does not is problematic as research suggests army partners and personnel rely primarily on friends and family for support.

Alienation and stigma

Relationships with civilians are complex but army partners regularly report feeling alienated during interaction. In my interviews, army partners regularly recount that when 'opening up' about military-related stress, they can be met with indifference by civilian friends and colleagues. They are told 'He knew what he was signing up for' and 'You made your bed, now lie in it'. These sentiments echo Congresswoman Frederica Wilson's accusation that President Donald Trump told recently widowed Myeshia Johnson that 'He knew what he was signing up for, but I guess it hurts anyway'.

Army partners tire of explaining themselves, especially when met with ambivalence from civilians who lack understanding about wider implications. In talking about her experiences before the return of her partner from deployment, one partner said:

'They can be coming home in two weeks and you can phone up and have a complete meltdown to military friends and sob and sob and sob, and just say I feel miserable today, I've just had enough. Whereas someone else will say, "Oh, they're coming home in two weeks, you must be happy".'

The return of the soldier is not a return to stability – relationship building is necessary and redeployment is always on the horizon.

Another army partner said her civilian friends have the same level of understanding as her toddler. It was also reported that civilians compare deployment to shorter separations like work conferences – disregarding risk to life and that deployments are lengthy. Some army partners also felt that civilians unfairly stigmatised the military community for being unruly and aggressive.

Disregard and ambivalence alienates army partners from the wider community and makes it difficult for them to seek support. As more military families are expected to live among the civilian community, it is essential that understanding of serving families' daily realities are developed. Civilians need to learn to empathise and not to pity to ensure military partners do not become isolated members of our communities.

9 November 2018

Do ex-soldiers need more help returning to 'civvy street'?

By Sophie Smith

James Stevenson is one of the thousands of former military personnel to have traded guns, barracks and patrols for computers, meetings and tea runs.

The transition from the Army, where Stevenson enjoyed a 36-year career as a brigadier, to Deloitte could not have been more straightforward for the married father-of-two.

Networking helped him find the role in the accounting giant's tax department, which began with a two-week placement in summer 2016 before being offered a full-time role. 'There were two considerations for me when choosing a job: to work with people I fit in with, and to join a large, respectable organisation that I could feel proud to work for,' he says.

'I had the most fantastically fun and fulfilling military career, and I ticked all the boxes I wanted to tick. But at the age of 55 they politely showed me the door and I had to make a choice about my future employment. While the thought of jumping ship into a brave new world was daunting, I had a lot of help and support in getting a job I enjoy.'

But not all veterans can relate to Stevenson's experience of a seamless transition back to 'civvy street', or civilian life.

Wayne Taylor, who served in the army for 25 years and did tours of duty in Afghanistan, Bosnia, Kosovo and Northern Ireland, has spoken of his battle to find work after applying for 400 jobs because he did not have relevant experience.

'The trouble with trying to get work if you're ex-army is they look at us and think we were only there to kill people – that's putting it bluntly but it's how it is. It's not easy,' he said in 2017.

One of the biggest challenges faced by the 16,000 people who leave the military every year is convincing employers that their skills and experiences are applicable in the business world. Many will not have had a job interview since joining the forces as teenagers, may never have written a CV and are unlikely to have any experience in the industry they want to enter.

The Ministry of Defence (MoD) maintains that the employment rate of former service personnel is in line with the average for the general population, at about 79%. That figure is backed by a 2018 Deloitte survey which found eight in ten veterans were in paid employment after leaving the armed forces.

However, the same survey showed that one in five veterans described the process of finding the right role as 'very difficult', with a lack of experience the biggest hurdle. Ex-military personnel often complain of the difficulties in finding 'meaningful and satisfying' work that the headline employment statistic does not necessarily reflect.

Given the majority of service leavers are from the army (the largest part of the armed forces), which is known to recruit young people from more deprived backgrounds with poor educational qualifications, it is easy to see why many find it difficult to secure skilled, well-paid work as a civilian.

A 2014 consultation from St George's House and the Forces in Mind Trust proposed that, by 2020, every member of the services should have a 'personal pathway of advice and support' that from recruitment onwards 'prepares them for a successful transition into civilian life'. The principle of 'personalising' pathways would mean that the MoD no longer follows 'a sheep-dip approach' to preparing service personnel for transition, it said.

Last year the government launched a consultation called 'Strategy for our veterans' in which it said that those leaving the armed forces face 'distinct challenges compared to their civilian counterparts in entering employment'.

'The MoD recognises the need to enable its people to secure further employment, should they want it, once they leave the regular services. As part of the defence resettlement policy… everyone who has decided to leave the armed forces [is offered] access to one-to-one guidance, training and employment opportunities for two years following exit, based on an eligibility related to length of service,' it stated.

The paper concluded that the onus was on the government to 'assist employers in recognising the value and expertise that veterans offer'.

Deloitte is one of a number of firms to offer civilian careers to those leaving the armed forces. At any one time it has about 200 veterans working across the UK business in departments such as cybersecurity, tax, consulting and risk advisory.

National Rail, Barclays, Rentokil, Amazon and Boeing – where veterans represent 15% of the plane maker's 20,000-strong UK workforce – are among the other firms to actively recruit ex-forces.

These companies speak of the transferable skills and attributes that a former soldier can bring to a role, such as discipline, leadership, teamwork, and the ability to stay calm under pressure.

But many businesses continue to overlook their value. Deloitte's survey found that three in ten UK companies admit they have not considered employing veterans, while 60% would rule out recruiting someone if they had no industry-specific experience – thus excluding most veterans.

Conservative MP and former British army officer Johnny Mercer says that companies should 'absolutely' be less rigid with their hiring criteria and more open to recognising the value ex-forces can bring to an organisation.

'The employment rate for ex-armed forces should be 100%, not 80%. Military life prepares you well for employment as a civilian, and employers do recognise this, but there should be more support from the government when it comes to their transition from service to civvy street,' he says. 'There needs to be more focus on what specific challenges veterans face when returning to work.'

Rob Crowe joined the army aged 17 and left five and a half years later to 'take back control of his life'. He found low-skilled, low-paid work a week after his departure and bounced from job to job for months before finding long-term work at pest control firm Rentokil in 2013.

'It was a bit of a nightmare when I left the army to be honest. I found a few low-paid jobs online – I basically took anything that was available – but only lasted a month at each place. I felt like I didn't fit in,' he says.

'The help in transitioning into civilian life wasn't very good. We had one Career Transition Partnership workshop (the programme that helps ex-service people find civilian careers) for half a day and were told to log into a computer to find advice and tips on choosing a career. There was no other direction.'

2.5 million

The number of veterans in Britain. This is projected to decrease to 1.6 million by 2028.

Crowe, who is now 29, says there should be more support given to veterans, many of whom joined the military as teenagers and 'don't know anything about civilian life'. He adds: 'They should teach ex-soldiers independence. We are trained to follow orders and do as they say, so we're not used to having independence and using our intuition to find work.'

Stevenson says he had a more positive experience with army support. Five years before he was due to leave he was given the option to attend a career transition workshop, where he was provided with 'top-grade teaching and mentoring, with resources that were generous and helpful. I definitely had a lot of support, in fact it was more than I could cope with. The challenge is utilising that support,' he says.

Lee Holloway, chief executive of the Officers' Association, which helps veterans and their families transition back to civilian life, says that while government support for veterans is available, it is a 'one-size-fits-all model' and that there 'can always be more' assistance provided.

The association works with about four in five people who leave the armed forces, giving them career options and putting them in contact with mentors and employers. Holloway says while many large businesses recruit veterans, it is harder to communicate the value of employing ex-forces to small and medium-sized companies.

Crowe believes more employers should be open to hiring military personnel because they are among the 'most loyal and hardworking' people in the country: 'If you tell an ex-soldier to do something, they'll do it.'

3 June 2019

Veterans should not be presented as a sub-species of society

Veterans should not be turned into icons of abandonment, says Veterans Aid.

Yesterday a Veterans in Custody officer from a prison contacted Veterans Aid to ask about support for veterans on discharge. The officer gave the impression that this was a serious problem. Naturally we asked how many in the system claimed to be veterans and the number quoted was 15 out of 610… a little under 2.5%. Of course, none of these claims of service were verified and that is a concern. We had previously worked with a major prison to verify military service claims by those in its care. In the end it emerged that 50% of those claiming military service in that prison had never served.

Recent examples of this relate to homelessness/rough sleeping and mental health – despite a worrying lack of hard evidence to support claims that veterans are at uniquely 'high risk' of either.

On 28th June 2019 *Support for UK Veterans* was published, a House of Commons Briefing Paper detailing the support available to armed forces veterans in Great Britain and Northern Ireland. The statistics it cites relating to health, employment, home ownership, etc. are positive and confirm what Veterans Aid has been saying for many years – i.e. that veterans are generally robust and resilient – but it makes some sweeping assumptions about other issues that must be challenged.

The briefing paper records that *'It has long been recognised that ex-service personnel are at a higher risk of experiencing* street homelessness than the civilian population' and refers to the latest CHAIN database. This records that, over the year, 362 people (i.e. 7% of those seen rough sleeping in London, in 2017/18) claimed that they had experience of serving in the armed forces. However, only 135 were UK nationals - none of whom had their claims of service verified. In a city of 8.7 million people, this is not a high number.

Having first-hand knowledge of fake claims of service among the homeless, coupled with dealing with the issue of rough sleeping on a daily basis, I must even question the number of 135 over the year. But the language used in the report isn't helpful and belittles the superb work being done by the military charity sector with regards to homelessness. I've been involved with veteran homelessness for 25 years and I have never seen any evidence that veterans are at higher risk. Indeed, I would argue that the positive life benefits related to military service go a long way to ensuring veterans do not end up on our streets. I think the author would struggle to prove the claim of higher risk.

We know from frequent discourse with the data gatherers that this putative military service is neither verified nor examined in context.

Another example of language used in the report that can lead to misinterpretation is where it claims that *'Links have been made between mental ill health and rough sleeping amongst ex-service personnel.'* It doesn't say by whom and it

does not add that there are links between mental health and rough sleeping/homelessness in the general population. The language used suggests a causal link between military service and mental health among rough sleepers which I think is a very misleading.

As a key and highly experienced frontline agency with street homeless veterans we have seen no evidence to back up this link. However, there is ample evidence of general poor mental health among street dwellers.

Mental health is simply not a 'military malady'; for example, a recent BMJ survey, reported in *Politics Home*, revealed that MPs were *'more likely to suffer depression, unhappiness and worthlessness than the general public'*.

The two important issues that we seem to be forgetting are verification and context. Because of the regard and status that veterans enjoy in the UK it is important that they are represented honestly. They number more than two million; their ages and life experiences are wide ranging and diverse; they are not an homogenous unit, yet they continue to have societal ills uniquely assigned to them as though a wider context did not exist.

Research by the Institute for Fiscal Studies, funded by JRF, indicates that between 1994 and 2017 there was an increase from 13% to 18% in the proportion of people in working households living in relative poverty (that's an increase of 40%). So, by 2017 eight million people in the UK, living in working households, were in relative poverty. Inevitably, some will be veterans.

Poverty leads to debt, mental health problems, relationship breakdown and social isolation. Many of the ex-servicemen and women seeking help from Veterans Aid are members of the working poor. The fact that they are veterans is largely irrelevant and they should not be turned into icons of abandonment.

It is entirely right that help is made available to veterans who are homeless, unemployed, unwell and in adversity and, as

Support for UK Veterans illustrates, aid is there aplenty. But as Adrian Massey pointed out in *The Guardian* recently, 'Not all suffering is mental illness. Pretending it is raises false hopes and puts pressure on an already strained NHS'. He is not talking about veterans per se, but his conclusion about an excessively medicalised approach to mental health being neither humane nor kind is relevant. He says, 'It fosters a learned helplessness, seeding doubt in the mind of the individual about their ability to endure life without the relentless input of doctors. Many form unhealthy, dependent relationships with healthcare professionals while becoming isolated from the kind of practical, amateur, human support that in many cases would be more helpful'.

Sadly, veterans' issues can be easily hijacked to serve any topical cause; their involvement provides an immediate halo effect to the man (or woman) who calls 'foul' on their behalf. Using frequently unverified statistics that provoke knee-jerk reactions of outrage is not helpful and provides ammunition to those who exploit. Veterans should not be presented as a sub-species of society. Labelling everyday problems as military-related issue is patently wrong. We should start thinking of veterans simply as fellow members of society with shared hopes, fears, rights, aspirations – and problems! And while we may not have a perfect veterans support system, frontline observations illustrate that if you are in crisis in Britain today, you are singularly lucky to be a veteran.

A good example is the campaign presently being run by the Royal Air Force Benevolent Fund to reach out to 100,000 veterans.

8 July 2019

Female veterans feel less supported on Civvy Street than their male equivalents

Female veterans feel less supported than their male counterparts after their military service, research from SSAFA, the Armed Forces charity has revealed.

The YouGov survey[1] which was issued as part of the charity's report *The Nation's Duty* found that almost half (46%) of female veterans in the UK felt that the support for male veterans is better than for female veterans. Almost as many (43%) reported feeling on their own with no one looking out for them after they hung up their uniform.

This research is reflected in the increased number of women coming forward asking to be matched with an SSAFA mentor. Currently, female mentees make up 22% of people requesting the service, which is disproportionate to the male and female (90%/10%), split of the Armed Forces.[2]

The SSAFA mentoring service provides one-to-one support for service leavers and their families during the pivotal transition back to civilian life. SSAFA mentors help with practical and emotional support, assisting with decision making, supporting career decisions and offering independent and confidential advice.

When questioned about their experiences, over a third of former servicewomen (35%) said they weren't fully prepared for civilian life. Further to this, 38% of female veterans said they did not plan their post-military career before they left the Armed Forces. Although many service leavers thrive in civilian life, if a veteran is struggling and the issues are not addressed early enough, they can escalate to a stage where more drastic intervention may be necessary.

These veterans may later re-emerge needing the charity's support. SSAFA mentoring service looks to address whether this could be avoided by providing early preventative support.

Gary Williams, Head of SSAFA's Mentoring Service, said:

'Whilst it's concerning that female veterans don't feel they are getting the right support, it is reassuring that we continue to see a rise in former servicewomen approaching SSAFA to be paired with a mentor.

'Currently, female serving personnel make up just under 10% of the Armed Forces, but with close combat roles being opened to women recruits, it's possible we will see a further increase in the demand for our service.

'All servicewomen, female veterans and female spouses are eligible for our support services including SSAFA mentoring and we would encourage anyone facing difficult times to get in touch.'

The Military Times Comment:

The raw statistics would appear to provide a rather gloomy view of the support available to women, but they warrant a much closer examination of the facts to see where and how the perception has grown amongst female veterans that they are less cared-for than men. From the outset, it has to be emphasised that this is to do with the support provided generally after leaving, and not specifically about problems such as front-line PTSD, which one might assume would currently apply less to most women in the forces than men, though an obvious exception might be amongst those who served with medical units in the Gulf or Afghanistan, for example.

The next question would be where the failures occur. Is it within the Armed Forces in the period prior to leaving, or is it with the support received after leaving and while out in Civvy Street looking for jobs, housing and other support. If the former, then it points to a clear problem within the military system; if the latter, it might be more problematic to solve.

Thirdly, it has to be asked what sort of support is felt to be missing. It might be that the support is there – but it is not the 'right' support. In which case, it has to be asked whether actual needs differ between men and women, or whether perceptions of what is on offer differ sufficiently to have to re-package, rather than re-organise, what is being made available. For example, are resettlement courses aimed predominantly at male occupations in Civvy Street, or are those intended for women not properly advertised?

The whole question of why women should feel less supported is concerning because, by relying upon organisations such as SSAFA, the 'buck' has been effectively passed by the MOD to charitable organisations – which is wrong by any reckoning. If there is a systemic problem, then the system has to be modified to deal with it on a systematic basis – and by the MOD.

There is another issue here, which is that there is a tendency in this modern world to try to pretend that men and women are all the same. We are not, and this is a good example of how a system that is intended to deal with 'a veteran' is actually not completely fit for purpose and that someone in the MOD has to ask why such a high proportion of women leaving the Armed Forces should feel so let down. Perhaps a study is underway – in which case it would be very interesting to hear from anyone who has been interviewed about this matter.

19 September 2018

1. YouGov survey was based on the responses of a panel of 251 veterans, aged 18–45, answering an online questionnaire.

2. Female serving personnel currently make up 10% of the Armed Forces.

www.themilitarytimes.co.uk

www.ssafa.org.uk

Ex-female soldiers asked if they can act feminine during job interview

Gender inequality is a passé problem but it's still present and this becomes crystal clear with Barclays research that shows the difficulties female veterans face getting a job.

By Varsha Saraogi

It's hardly a secret companies have stereotypes for women while recruiting. Remember that time a receptionist was sent packing from PwC for not having heels on? But business heads have been harbouring too many prejudiced ideas for female veterans in particular.

This was backed by a study done by Barclays' Armed Forces Transition, Employment & Resettlement (AFTER) programme, which shed light on the bias companies have against ex-female soldiers when they apply for a job.

Of the 502 veterans surveyed, 42% of females said they felt their military background was the reason they hadn't been offered job interviews or taken through to next stages of the application process, according to the report. For those who did get through, one in three faced questions on whether they knew how to act and dress in a femininely. Further to this, while 39% of male veterans found a job within a month, this was true for only 21% of women.

To counter the problem, 44% of ex-female soldiers took on additional training to feel more competent, which fell to 28% for men – a testament of the gender disparity company leaders are guilty of ignoring.

While women have been successful to break the glass ceiling in combat, businesses haven't advanced their attitudes to cater to female veterans' employment needs. There has been an increase of women in the army who make up 10.3% of the UK regular forces; however, it seems the transition to a civilian lifestyle is a challenging mountain to scale. And being discriminated against only makes that slope more slippery.

Commenting on businesses stereotyping ex-military women, Stuart Tootal, head of the Barclays AFTER programme, said: 'It's disappointing to see that female veterans are being overlooked and having to go the extra mile when transitioning into a civilian career. We must all play our part and take action to level this playing field – businesses must provide more support to veterans of both sexes and fully recognise the very real talent that they can add to any organisation.'

From struggling to stay alive whilst protecting the nation to getting a paycheque for putting food on the table – the difficulties a female veteran has cannot be fathomed and businesses definitely need to be more inclusive.

19 July 2018

250,000 veterans helped into new careers

The Ministry of Defence's Career Transition Partnership celebrates its 20th anniversary.

In the two decades since its launch, a quarter of a million service leavers have been supported in the next stage of their careers by the Career Transition Partnership (CTP), a partnership between the MOD and Right Management Ltd.

The CTP offers one-to-one career guidance, vocational training, events, networking and employment opportunities to serving personnel for up to two years before they leave the Armed Forces, supporting them as they prepare to enter the civilian workplace or further education.

Benefitting from training in interview techniques and CV development, as well as targeted workshops designed to identify and harness an individual's strengths, 93% of service leavers transitioning through the CTP who are seeking employment, are in new roles within six months.

Ex-serving personnel can also access CTP support for two years after they have transitioned back into civilian life, ensuring the adjustment process is as smooth as possible.

Tobias Ellwood, Minister for Defence People and Veterans, said:

Our Armed Forces develop invaluable, lasting and transferable skills during their service, and it is right that we support them to reach their potential when they leave.

With admirable qualities such as leadership, dedication and team work, those who have served are an asset to any organisation. The CTP team plays an evermore vital role in helping our people navigate the many opportunities open to them.

The CTP also provides specialist training to those who leave service early through the Future Horizons programme, which has supported 11,500 personnel since its introduction in 2008. A further specialised career programme, CTP Assist, supports approximately 900 wounded, injured and sick service leavers per year to achieve a sustainable and fulfilling career, regardless of time served.

The CTP offers a wide range of vocational training courses to enhance qualifications gained in the military or to retrain for a new career. Courses in fields such as finance, project management, IT and health and safety, and are designed around the needs of service leavers and to connect with routes to employment.

The CTP Employment Team is focused on engaging with local SMEs and national employers to create unique pathways into employment and ensuring organisations take a strategic approach to integrate military talent into their workforce planning.

The CTP is currently working closely with a broad range of employers such as Amazon, Barclays, Jaguar Land Rover, BAE Systems, and Openreach to align the wealth of transferable skills and experiences service leavers have.

Along with online career resettlement guides, personnel can also access advice on wider aspects of the transition process, including housing and pensions, managing finances, and moving abroad. This guidance is part of the broader support on offer to personnel to bridge the gap between military and civilian life.

The CTP is the first example of a military resettlement service provided by a partnership of private, public and charitable organisations, anywhere in the world. The model, established by the partnership between the MOD and Right Management Ltd, is supported by RFEA – The Forces Employment Charity, who deliver CTP's employment support, and is at the forefront of best international practice.

David Duffy, Right Management Ltd, Contract Director for Career Transition Partnership, said:

I' am proud that Right Management have delivered a world-class resettlement provision on behalf of the MOD for two decades, helping to bridge the gap between military and civilian careers and connecting Armed Forces personnel to jobs. CTP staff are extremely committed and passionate about the part they play in supporting service leavers and this is evident in the remarkable achievements we have made.

'The working landscape has changed beyond all recognition since we started, with an ever more transient marketplace and technology, along with social media, driving change at pace. Despite this, the CTP has stayed at the forefront of delivery, keeping pace with change and continually adapting to meet the needs of our service leavers.'

12 October 2018

Case study: banking on ex-military talent

Barclays is making the transition from military to 'civvy street' employment as smooth as possible for UK veterans.

By Rachel Sharp

The organisation

Barclays is an investment banking and financial services company founded in the UK more than 300 years ago. As of April 2018, Barclays Bank UK (the UK division) and Barclays Bank (made up of the group service company and Barclays International) operate independently but alongside one another as part of Barclays plc. The group has operations in 40-plus countries and employs around 120,000 people.

The problem

Changing company, job role, or career is a challenging time for anyone. But for someone who has spent the entirety of their adult life in the military and has left – often because of injury – these challenges are amplified.

'I thought I was a career soldier. I was in infantry for ten years, did three tours of Iraq, and picked up an injury that led to me being medically discharged,' explains Kevin Gartside, Barclays' Armed Forces Transition, Employment and Resettlement (AFTER) programme manager.

'I found myself in a position where I had no idea what I wanted to do and – apart from the army aptitude test – had never had a job interview in my life.'

Gartside's story is far from unique. Research from the British Legion shows that working-age veterans are almost twice as likely to be unemployed as their counterparts in the UK general population.

As Gartside explains, there are several factors (both work-related and personal) holding veterans back when it comes to reintegrating into civilian employment.

'It's such a change in lifestyle as well as a change in job,' he says. 'You're finding your feet in life again because you're moving out of what is a very protective culture. So it's not just about integrating into traditional work life but also back into "normal" life.'

Skills transfer is another issue. 'Military people aren't very good at translating their military skillset into the civilian world and civilian workplaces also have a poor understanding of the skills that someone in the military can bring to an organisation,' Gartside adds.

'Biases also need to be dispelled. Hiring managers will often ask really inappropriate questions like "have you killed anyone?"'

The stereotypes employers have of veterans, coupled with the limited awareness veterans have for the types of roles they could move into, means valuable transferable skills are going untapped by businesses. According to the Barclays Military Insight Tool veterans outperform civilians in a number of areas; scoring in the top 30% for social influence, creativity, rational decision-making, emotional resilience and dealing with ambiguity.

Clearly overlooking veterans as prospective employees isn't just a CSR matter. It's also causing employers to miss out on a highly talented demographic of workers at a time they can scarce afford to do so.

The method

Barclays' AFTER programme was set up in 2010. Launched by Stuart Tootal, head of Barclays' AFTER programme and a former army colonel, it started as an informal side job alongside his security role at the bank.

'It began by providing employability grants to help wounded, injured, sick and vulnerable service veterans develop long-term careers,' explains Gartside. This quickly evolved into Barclays staff running employability training and CV workshops. But it wasn't perfect from the get-go.

'Barclays staff were running a workshop and some veterans told them it wasn't good. So to make the programme actually suit their needs and be effective we got them to help us create it,' says Gartside.

Giving a standard CV template to someone who may never have written one before and who doesn't know how to translate their military experiences to 'civvy street' won't work. Instead the plan shifted to running two-day workshops allowing veterans time to develop the skills to write a CV, conduct interview practice and, perhaps more importantly, rebuild confidence.

Further to the CV workshops, the programme expanded to include insight days to give veterans firsthand experience of working in banking, two-week placements in Barclays, and then the launch of a 12-week Barclays Military Internship

programme in 2015. Gartside explains that this internship is open to people in the last six months of service where they can usually 'manage their time away from the chain of command but are still being paid by the military'.

As part of the internship they are given a line manager, a military mentor or 'buddy', access to all Barclays' systems, and a role in the bank. Interns are given access to Barclays' internal jobs boards and classed as internal candidates to then apply for permanent roles. The support doesn't end after onboarding, with ongoing access to a military support network and Barclays mentors assigned.

Not all mentors are ex-servicemen and women, Gartside adds, but 'veterans supporting veterans' is a winning formula in many cases. 'Just having someone to have a coffee with [who can] tell you they've been through the same thing and succeeded helps.'

It hasn't all been plain sailing, however. Shifting the mindset of existing employees brings its own challenges.

Gartside explains that some parts of the business were more open to the idea than others. Functions such as risk and security seemed more obvious homes for veterans' skills than CSR or investment banking for example.

'It was a slow build,' he says. 'It is as much of an education and training piece for line managers and hiring managers as for veterans.' As such the programme also provides line managers with briefing packs containing tips on what to expect; from military acronyms to awareness around where additional training and support may be required.

'It's about reminding them that some veterans may be more nervous on their first day in a bank than they would be in Iraq,' Gartside adds.

And it's not just about recruiting into Barclays itself; 2015 saw the launch of Veterans Employment Transition Support (VETS), aimed at helping other organisations connect with ex-service personnel, as well as providing veterans access to mentors from other businesses and the chance to apply for targeted job opportunities. All in all it's about making the transition as smooth as possible.

The result

Having joined Barclays in 2012 on a placement in what was then the programme in its informal infancy, and then being accepted into a full-time role at the bank – before joining the AFTER programme team in 2014 – Gartside's own story is testament to its success.

To date Barclays has helped more than 5,000 service personnel in the transition process and employed more than 500 ex-military staff internally in the bank. The employment piece is a point of particular pride, with a 90% conversion rate of interns to full-time employees. This ranges across all levels of seniority, from junior analysts to senior directors, and across all parts of the business.

'There's no limit – if everyone hits the mark and wants to stay at Barclays then we find them a role,' says Gartside.

He also estimates that around 90% of the veterans Barclays has hired through the programme would never have considered a career in banking if they hadn't been exposed to the opportunities and range of roles there.

While the programme is constantly growing and evolving, with plans to roll out the model in Barclays' US markets, the key to its success for Gartside has been a human touch. 'It's not done on a scale of 20,000 people at a time as we'd lose the fact it is very human,' he says.

Nevertheless, perhaps one of the biggest markers of success is the high demand from the business for the kinds of diverse skills ex-military personnel can bring. As Gartside explains: 'We used to be asking if teams wanted an intern, but now it's the other way around.'

2 August 2018

www.hrmagazine.co.uk

Key facts

- The total strength of the full-time UK Armed Forces (trained and untrained) at 1 April 2019 was just under 153,000. (page 1)

- At 1 October 2018 there were 15,260 women in the UK Regular Forces and accounted for 11% of the total trained and untrained strength. (page 1)

- As of 1 October 2018 around 8% of personnel (10,950) identified as belonging to a non-white ethnic group. (page 2)

- In the US, 50% of Americans say that everyone serving in the armed forces is a hero, regardless of their role or experience. (page 3)

- In the UK, 32% consider all armed forces personnel to be heroes. (page 3)

- In Germany, the most common response was that no members of the armed forces should be described as heroes. (page 3)

- In the UK and Germany it is the younger generations who are most likely to believe that all who serve in the armed forces are heroes. (page 3)

- A National Audit Office report found the number of full-time military personnel, known as regulars, was 5.7%, or 8,200 people, short of the required level. (page 5)

- Only 7% of people know someone who is currently serving in the forces. (page 6)

- The size of the armed forces is about 9,000 below target. (page 7)

- In the year to June 2018 around 12,000 personnel joined the UK Regular Forces, and around 15,000 left– altogether a loss of around 3,000 people. (page 7)

- After the recent recruitment campaign applications to join the army rose to 9,700 – a five-year high. (page 8)

- One in four soldiers in the UK army is under 18. (page 9)

- The British armed forces recruit around 2,300 16- and 17-year-olds each year, of whom four-fifths join the army. (page 10)

- Three-quarters of 16-year-old recruits have a reading age of 11 or less. (page 10)

- Armed forces personnel across all ranks and ages are twice as likely as civilians to suffer from anxiety and depression and 50 percent more likely to experience PTSD. (page 11)

- It costs £53,000 to train an adult for the infantry, but £103,500 to train a minor for the same role to the same standard. (page 11)

- Until 2016, women were not permitted to serve in ground close combat roles at all. (page 12)

- The MOD has also set a target of 10% of recruits being from BAME backgrounds by 2020. (page 16)

- Over a third of the UK do not actively support the Armed Forces, rising to 48% for those aged 16–34. (page 20)

- 52% are more familiar with the roles of the Armed Forces while engaged in active conflict, than they are now. (page 20)

- 50% of the public are unaware of where our Forces are based in the world, with 16% mistakenly believing the majority to still be in Afghanistan. (page 20)

- 58% know more about historical military events, such as D-Day, than they do about our current military. (page 20)

- The Ministry of Defence spends £22 million a year on mental healthcare for veterans. (page 23)

- Suicide is currently the biggest killer of men under the age of 45 in the Western world. (page 23)

- In 2018, research by a Scottish newspaper demonstrated that a former member of the forces takes their own life in Scotland every six days. (page 23)

- About 11% of men and 5% of women in the UK armed forces meet the criteria for alcohol misuse. (page 26)

- The fees for indefinite leave to remain have risen by 127% in five years to £2,389 per person, amounting to almost £10,000 for a family of four. Since their introduction in 2003, the fees have risen by 1,441%. (page 28)

- In 2017, around 7.1% of army recruits were from Commonwealth countries. (page 28)

- Army families living in military accommodation during the working week have decreased from 76% in 2010 to 68% in 2017. (page 29)

- Three in ten UK companies admit they have not considered employing veterans. (page 31)

- 50% of those claiming military service in a major prison had never served. (page 32)

- 7% of those seen rough sleeping in London, in 2017/18 claimed that they had experience of serving in the armed forces. (page 32)

- 46% of female veterans in the UK felt that the support for male veterans is better than for female veterans. (page 34)

- Over a third of former servicewomen (35%) said they weren't fully prepared for civilian life. (page 34)

- 42% of females said they felt their military background was the reason they hadn't been offered job interviews. (page 36)

Armed Forces

The Armed Forces consists of the Army (the British Army consists of Regular Forces and Volunteer Reserves), naval service (the Royal Navy and the Royal Marines) and the Royal Air Force. The purpose of these military forces is to strengthen international peace and security.

Armed Forces Covenant

The Armed Forces Covenant sets out the relationship between the nation, the Government and the armed forces. The covenant exists to redress the disadvantages that the armed forces community may face in comparison to other citizens, and to recognise sacrifices made. The covenant's two principles are that: the armed forces community should not face disadvantage compared to other citizens in the provision of public and commercial services; and special consideration is appropriate in some cases, especially for those who have given most, such as the injured and the bereaved.

AWOL

This stands for 'absent without leave'. It refers to a serviceperson who has absented themselves from their military duties without the appropriate permission to do so.

Civilian

Anyone who is not a member of the military.

Civvy street

An informal phrase sometimes used by servicepeople and veterans to describe life and work outside of the military ('civvy' being short for 'civilian').

Close combat

In a battle situation, this refers to fighting between two combatants at short range.

Deployment

The movement of military personnel into an area of operation (such as a combat zone).

Discharge (from the armed forces)

A discharge is given to a member of the Armed Forces when their obligation to serve is over, releasing them from duty. There are different types of discharge, including Honourable and Dishonourable.

Leave (from the armed forces)

A serviceperson's paid holiday allowance – 38 days' holiday per year is the minimum for soldiers - is referred to as 'leave'.

Mental health/wellbeing

Everyone has 'mental health'. It includes our emotional, psychological and social wellbeing. It affects how we think, feel, and act. It also helps determine how we handle stress, relate to others, and make choices. Mental health is important at every stage of life, from childhood and adolescence through adulthood.

Military ethos

This spirit of the military; this refers to characteristics such as building character, resilience, self-discipline and teamwork.

Millenials

Often referred to as Generation Y, millennials are typically born between the early 1980s and the early 2000s. This generation is associated with a familiarity of digital technology, communications and media.

Operations

Military actions in response to a developing situation or crisis.

Post-Traumatic Stress Disorder (PTSD)

PTSD is a psychological reaction to a highly traumatic event. It has been known by different names at different times in history: during the First World War, for example, soldiers suffering from PTSD were said to have 'shell shock'.

Regulars

Soldiers and officers of the regular Army ('regulars') are full-time military personnel. The regulars are distinct from those who serve in the Territorial Army, who train in their spare time.

Territorial Army

Territorial soldiers and officers train in their spare time to provide support to full-time regular units when they're needed. There are two types of Territorial Unit – Regional and National. Regional Units train on week nights and some weekends and recruit from the local area. National Units tend to be more specialised and recruit people with relevant experience from all over the country. Because members travel further to get to training, they don't train on week nights. Most Army jobs are open to Territorials.

Veteran

A former serving member of the Armed Forces, in particular one who has given service during conflict or in time of war (more widely, the term 'veteran' is sometimes applied to anyone who has had long service in a particular field – people often talk about 'a veteran actor', for example).

Activities

Brainstorming

◆ In small groups, discuss what you know about the Armed Forces. Consider the following points:

- What services does the Armed Forces in the UK consist of?

- What do the Armed Forces do?

- What is the Territorial Army?

- What does 'military ethos' mean to you?

Research

◆ Find out about the condition of PTSD throughout history, beginning in the First World War. How was 'shell shock' diagnosed and treated? How has the way this illness is perceived changed since the early years of the 20th century? Do you think there is still a degree of stigma attached to this problem? Write a summary of your research findings.

◆ Do some research into where the armed forces are currently based. Choose one location and find out what they are responding to and how they are helping to resolve the situation.

◆ Do some research on ways that the armed forces help out in times of need in the UK.

◆ Create a questionnaire on attitudes to the armed forces – consider the different branches of the forces and see if there is any difference in attitudes to them. Or, the difference in attitudes between different age groups.

◆ Do some research into different careers that are available within the forces.

◆ Do some research into charities and organisations in the UK that support our forces.

Design

◆ Design a poster that will raise awareness of the role of the Armed Forces.

◆ Design a leaflet offering advice to someone leaving the forces. Include some organisations or charities that offer help to veterans.

◆ Choose one of the articles in this topic and create an illustration to highlight the key themes/message of your chosen article.

◆ Design a poster to celebrate armed forces day.

◆ Choose one of the articles in this book and create an infographic to display the key points/facts.

◆ Design a poster to promote wellbeing in the forces.

Oral

◆ 'People under the age of 18 should not be able to join the armed forces.' Debate this motion as a class, with one group arguing in favour and the other against.

◆ The mental health of the Armed Forces is a big issue. Do some research on the matter and create a three-minute presentation that explores your findings and share this with your class. You could include images, videos, maps and statistics to engage your audience.

◆ As a class, discuss the role of women in the Armed Forces. Why is there so much controversy surrounding this issue? Should/can women be in combat roles? Why or why not?

◆ In small groups discuss mental health in the armed forces.

Reading/writing

◆ Write a one-paragraph definition of the Armed Forces.

◆ Write a poem, empathising with someone who has joined the forces.

◆ Imagine that you are going to interview a veteran. Write a list of five questions that you would like to ask them, and write a response for each question.

◆ Imagine you work for a charity which helps veterans integrate back into society (back to 'civvy street'). Write a blog-post for your charity's website explaining the issues surrounding veteran care and your feelings about the issue.

◆ Write a diary entry from the perspective of a military veteran. What do you think your future will be like? How do you feel? How do you feel about society?

◆ Write a fictionalised first-person account of life after leaving the military. Will your character have any issues finding a home or work? Do they have a family to return to?

◆ Read some war poetry. Analyse the themes, speaker, rhyme scheme and language used. What message do you think the author was trying to portray?

Acknowledgements

The publisher is grateful for permission to reproduce the material in this book. While every care has been taken to trace and acknowledge copyright, the publisher tenders its apology for any accidental infringement or where copyright has proved untraceable. The publisher would be pleased to come to a suitable arrangement in any such case with the rightful owner.

Images

Cover image courtesy of iStock. All other images courtesy of Pixabay and Unsplash except images on pages 9, 12, 13, 14, 27 & 29 courtesy of the Ministry of Defence, © Crown copyright 2019

Illustrations

Don Hatcher: pages 2 & 20. Simon Kneebone: pages 10 & 34. Angelo Madrid: pages 6 & 32.

Additional acknowledgements

With thanks to the Independence team: Shelley Baldry, Danielle Lobban, Jackie Staines and Jan Sunderland.

Tracy Biram

Cambridge, September 2019